SKULL
CRUSHERS

EMPOWERING GOD'S DAUGHTERS TO
BE THE WARRIORS HE CREATED THEM TO BE

BECCA RAMIREZ

First Paperback edition August, 2022

Manufactured in the United States of America

Scriptures referred to in this book are taken from the most up to date translations of the Holy Bible published by Zondervan Publishing House and provided online by biblegateway.com.

Published by Victory Vision Publishing and Consulting
www.victoryvision.org

Imprint: Becca Ramirez. Author
Fort Worth, TX

Paperback ISBN: 979-8-9865358-0-7
eBook ISBN: 979-8-9865358-1-4

DEDICATION

To my mom, who always told me I could do
whatever I set my mind to.
To my sister, who never made me feel like I was less than.
To my daughters, who continue to amaze me daily.
To every girl who was told she wasn't good enough
and to all those girls who were never given the chance.
God has given us a voice. He has called each of us by name. You
are loved and cherished. You are warriors.

CONTENTS

ACKNOWLEDGMENTS

All of my writing is a journey. God plants an initial idea and then I find myself flushing out that idea in my own life and walk with Him. It's growth and refining and includes surprises along the way. Skull Crushers is a work that I have been humbled by. Not only in the research and discovery, but in the support that was birthed along the way.

I want to begin by thanking the women I work and volunteer with at Gateway Church, specifically at the North Fort Worth Campus. Each of you has been so gracious as I've talked though different ideas and doctrine. You've offered wisdom and direction to ever-increasing bunny trails. And more than anything, your continued words of encouragement for me has meant more than I could ever express. Thank you for your prayers. Thank you for your prophetic words shared with me. Thank you for your love and friendship. You are a beautiful picture of what sisters in Christ look like.

Thank you, Victory Vision Publishing, for helping make this a reality. For Julie and the entire team, I'm so grateful that you were able to take my words and vision and bring it to life.

Thank you, Suzi, for always being my editor extraordinaire.

I also want to thank the Appalachian Christian Writer's Conference. When I submitted my first chapter for the Sparrow Award Contest, I was terrified. I didn't realize how much of a crossroads I was standing on, wavering in my belief in this project. When you called my name to receive the award, my spirit was renewed and the fire within me was relit. It reminded me that this project was not just some random thought, but that it was transformative and important in this time and this season.

Finally, I want to take a moment to thank my family.

To my parents (who bought my ticket to the writer's conference and have always been my rock), thank you. The fact that I can confidently say these words and trust how God speaks in my life is built on the foundation of faith you poured into. I'm so thankful for the wisdom and love you continually give. I love you both, to the moon and back.

To my three awesome kiddos: thank you for your patience with Mommy over the last couple years. You guys are my inspiration, my motivation, and my light. You make me want a better world for you to grow up in, but I know that God's plans for each of you are great and He chose this time and place especially for you. Trust in His leading and He will guide your steps every day of your lives. I love you so much!

And last, but certainly not least, to my husband. Kyle, your love and support for me is humbling. You are one the greatest examples of God's love for me. I can be confident in my role as an Ezer because I know that standing back-to-back with me is a strong man of God— my husband, my best friend, my love. Thank you for battling with me, for continuing to call out who God has created me to be, and for loving me so well. *Por siempre mi amor.*

INTRODUCTION

When I was growing up, I felt torn between two worlds. On one side, I was strong-willed and opinionated. I believed that anything a boy could do, so could I (anyone else suddenly start singing, "Anything you can do I can do better. I can do anything better than you"? Just me? Okay, moving on.) On the other side, particularly during my teenage years as I began dating, I wrestled with this idea of the "submissive woman." I read the verses I was taught were specifically about women, then, coupled with a few very "traditional" teachings on women's roles, I lost confidence in who I thought I was. I questioned whether my strong personality—which was often defined by others (particularly boys) as "too much"—was more hindrance than benefit. Because of that struggle, I fell into a cycle of self-doubt and passivity. In her book, "Half the Church," Carolyn Curtis James discusses this challenge as we in the West live in a predominantly egalitarian society (leadership is based on merit not gender) but the church remains inconsistent in its stance. She says, "In one world our contributions and expertise are welcomed and valued. In the church we are a subject of debate, and our gifts can be problematic, unwelcome, or allowed only limited use."[1]

Now married with three children, my two oldest being girls, I have an intense desire to change the narrative. I want all my children to be confident in who God created them to be and know that His love for them doesn't waiver depending on whether or not they have a Y chromosome. I want to teach my children an accurate understanding of the power of the Holy Spirit so that when they are filled, they can walk boldly in all the gifts—not just the few that tradition decided were acceptable options.

---

[1] James, Carolyn Curtis. "Half the Church," 159. Grand Rapids: Zondervan, 2010.

My journey to discover Ezer began with a teaching I heard at a Propel Activate conference fall of 2019. The ministry of Propel is all about equipping female leaders but this particular message took it a step further for me. Rather than simply giving me tools and confidence to lead, it stirred up the warrior spirit within me. It challenged me to step up to a God-ordained calling to actively battle the enemy in his schemes. No longer did I feel satisfied to simply teach about the gentler side of my faith, but to readily equip God's daughters so that they too will be ready to face the battles before them. The Bible tells us that we do not fight against flesh and blood. The Passion Translation says it this way, "Your hand-to-hand combat is not with human beings but with the highest principalities and authorities operating in rebellion under the heavenly realms. For they are a powerful class of demon-gods and evil spirits that hold this dark world in bondage." (Ephesians 6:12)

The enemy is actively attacking both men and women and we are all given authority over him! We are called to fight! It's not passive. It's not sweet and gentle. It's war and women are in the midst of it without being readily equipped. We weren't called to wait on the sidelines and the enemy doesn't care if that's what we've been told our entire lives. In fact, I believe that too is a scheme of the enemy. Women have been under attack since the garden and it's time for us to recognize that our identity as a daughter of God also classifies us as warriors.

This is in no way a means of attempting to "even the score" or "turn the tables" against my brothers in Christ. In the beginning, God ordained man and woman to rule the earth and act as His image bearers. This was something to be shared between us, not to pit us against one another. Carolyn Curtis James said, "Let us not miss God's original vision, namely, that *he is raising up his daughters to be leaders.*"[2] We are *both* called to be God's image bearers. Neither of us can fully accomplish this monumental task on our own, and we weren't designed to. When God said, "It isn't good for man to be alone," we need to recognize that it goes well beyond pairing him with a wife. If the main role for women is to be wife and mother, then over half of the girls in the church will be left out. What about those who are unmarried or who are unable—or choose not—to have children? Being a wife and mother are incredibly important, but they are not the sole callings for women in the church. God has called us to be His image bearers and represent Him to the world just as fervently as He has called men.

I'm on a journey to equip myself and my sisters around me as we step up to the front lines. The Victory is won, but the battle rages on and we're deep in its trenches. Join me as we look at the true understanding of our role as ezers, learn that the historical narrative is not as clear as we've been led to believe, and understand how God has already equipped us to be victorious in this spiritual war through the stories of women in scripture.

---

[2] Ibid, 77.

VI

CHAPTER ONE
A FIGHT FROM
THE BEGINNING
EZER | GENESIS 2

The first line in books may seem innocuous and incon-
sequential, but the good ones manage to engrave themselves
on the depths of who we are and who we become. At the
very least we can always easily recall the popular ones. They set the
mood and expectation for the rest of the book. They catch our
attention to draw us into the world on the pages and settle in our
hearts when we remember.

"It was the best of times, it was the worst of times, it was the age of
wisdom, it was the age of foolishness..." (Charles Dickens, *Tale of
Two Cities*)

"It is a truth universally acknowledged that a single man in
possession of a good fortune must be in want of a wife." (Jane
Austen, *Pride and Prejudice*)

"In a hole in the ground there lived a hobbit." (J.R.R. Tolkien, *The
Hobbit*)

"Mr and Mrs Dursley, of number four, Privet Drive, were proud to say that they were perfectly normal, thank you very much." (J.K. Rowling, *The Sorcerer's Stone*)

"Once there were four children whose names were Peter, Susan, Edmund, and Lucy. This story is about something that happened to them when they were sent away from London during the war because of the air-raids." (C.S. Lewis, *The Lion, the Witch, and the Wardrobe*)

But there are none so monumental as: "In the beginning God created the heavens and the earth" (Genesis 1:1). What makes this line even better is that this is not a work of fiction, but truth. The first chapter of Genesis literally builds the world we live in, written for us to see and experience in a way only the written word can. And the first line isn't even the pinnacle of the story—that's found in verse 26.

"Then God said, 'Let us make man in our image according to our likeness. They will rule the fish of the sea, the birds of the sky, the livestock, the whole earth, and the creatures that crawl on the earth.'" (Genesis 1:26, CSB)

God's creation of mankind and giving them dominion of His creation sets the scene for our lives today. It was His original and perfect plan. But somewhere along the way (hint, it's found in chapter three of Genesis), the plan is disrupted, and division is driven between God's perfect creations—man and woman.

The enemy slithered in and led them to question God and His goodness, and in turn to question the blessing of each other. In the beginning, God created them to be partners, equal shareholders, warriors bonded together in perfect harmony. God created woman, not as an afterthought to Adam, but as a perfect complement. She was created to be a helper, equal and adequate to himself. She was an ezer.

We're still created to be ezers. This isn't merely another title to add to our list of expectations. This is an honor and a call to the depth of our hearts of who He created us to be. But because of sin, because of the meddling of the enemy, this is also our battle cry. Women today have lost sight of this title and have settled for a marginalized role that God never intended for us. Just as the title of ezer was given to Eve, it is given to each and every one of us today. It is who we are—who He created us to be. And the fight against us is one that has existed from the very beginning.

WE ARE EQUAL.

When we read the story of creation in Genesis, we see it presented from two points. Chapter one is like your Cliff Notes summary. It allows us to see the highlights from each of the six days of creation and get an understanding of the main idea—particularly in regard to the role God intended for Mankind.

Then God said, "Let us make man in our image, according to our likeness. **They** will rule the fish of the sea, the birds of the sky, the livestock, the whole earth, and the creatures that crawl on the earth."

So God created man
in his own image;
he created him in the image of God;
he created **them** male and female.
God blessed **them**, and God said to **them**, "Be fruitful, multiply, fill the earth, and subdue it. Rule the fish of the sea, the birds of the sky, and every creature that crawls on the earth." (Genesis 1:26-28, CSB, *emphasis mine*)

In the beginning, God had plans for *them*, his created image bearers—both male and female. Dominion was given to *them*. The ruling over the animals and the role of caring for the earth was given to *them*. Not just man. Not only that, but the blessing of God wasn't given to Adam alone, it was given after Eve was created. They were blessed in this role together. But why? Many cultures would have us believe that women are a lesser creation—an afterthought. We're taught about all the amazing roles that men can have—particularly within the church or religion in general—but women seemed deigned to do nothing more than birth and raise the children. (Mind you, this is one of our greatest honors and a tremendous blessing. I'm more emphasizing the limitations placed on women as a whole when it comes to typical roles.) Typical roles for women in the church are limited to childcare or hospitality of some kind. These roles are not lesser by any means, but there are many who feel stifled by them. We want to help, and we want to serve, but we also want to exercise *all* of the gifts that God has given us, just like our brothers in Christ are able to do without thought.

The other piece of importance in what God is doing in these verses is that He is giving us a physical, tangible example of what will later be revealed as a spiritual truth. We find this throughout scripture—God will do something in the physical, something we can see and better understand, to set up an understanding for something He is doing in the spiritual. In this specific case, we see the spiritual act explained in Galatians, chapter three.

"For those of you who were baptized into Christ have been clothed with Christ. There is no Jew or Greek, slave or free, male and female; since you are all one in Christ Jesus" (Galatians 3:27-28, CSB).

God gave equal ownership of the earth to Adam and Eve to set the tone for the equal co-heirship He was giving through the blood of Jesus. We are one; we are equal. We are all equally created to be image bearers of God.

Image bearer is a phrase that has been overly spiritualized without a clear understanding of what it means. Sure, we're created in the image of God. So what? If we think of it in earthly terms, the point becomes a little clearer.

Let's imagine a physical king—not omnipresent like God—limited to being in one place at one time. He is a great king with a great kingdom. He rules from his castle situated in the heart of the land he oversees. Now, he is a good and kind king who often goes out into that village where his castle resides and interacts with his people. They know him on sight. They recognize his voice. They trust him to be a good king because they have interacted with him and experienced firsthand how he handles situations. Like I said, this is a great kingdom, so while the king rules from the central part of the land, there are villages and provinces that exist on the far corners of this king's land. They are too far away to see and interact with the king. They know nothing about him or his heart for his people. The king is wise. He knows he needs to remain where he is to handle the greatest threats and concerns but still wanting all his subjects to know him, he decides to send out image bearers. These regents are tasked with going to the villages on the outskirts of the kingdom and living life with the people there. While they are there, they are the physical representation of the king. By their actions, the people can see how the king would act. By their words, the people can hear how the king would sound. When the people look at the image bearers, they should see and understand who their king is and how he cares for them.

My first jobs were in customer service, both with retail as well as restaurants. Because of this I tend to be a little critical when I speak to employees meant to represent their company. Okay, maybe a little more than a little critical sometimes, but I think we can all agree that there are those who are incredibly gifted at good customer service and there are others who are clearly not. Recently, my husband wanted to try out a new restaurant but knew that—being new—it would likely have a bit of a wait. That wasn't a problem, but we did want to get an idea of how long the wait would be considering we would also have our three young (hungry) children with us. When he called, the first question was whether they take reservations. No, they didn't. Nothing crazy there. Then he followed that question with one I consider fairly normal, "what is your typical wait time around 6pm?" We weren't looking for an exact answer, merely an approximation. The young lady's response was, "I can't answer that."

"I'm sorry, what?"

"I can't answer that."

Looking at each other, completely bewildered, my husband kindly prodded, "Why not?"

Please understand, we aren't crazy-particular people. In general, we're easy going and understanding of a lot of things, but like I said: I worked in customer service, and I also worked for a season in the food industry. At no point in time have I ever been told they can't give me an average wait time for a weeknight. We all know it's an approximation. In fact, that can even be emphasized that the time they state could very easily change. But that's not what was done and while this is an example that my husband and I laugh over—just bewildered by the whole interaction—the point is that this single interaction caused us to seriously consider changing our minds about trying this restaurant.

The role as image bearer for God is significantly more important than simply representing a restaurant or a company. It can be the difference between someone wanting to know more about who we represent or turning away to something else.

We as women are equal image bearers of God. We are created in the image of God just as much as our male counterparts are. Yes, we were specially designed to give birth, but that blessing is another example of a physical reality pointing to a spiritual truth. We have the privilege of carrying and growing a child in our wombs. We are honored to give birth to a new life. We also are tasked with carrying and growing inspiration and encouragement in our hearts. We don't just give birth to physical children, but to promise, truth, and hope.

WE ARE PRECIOUS VESSELS.

There are many who love and honor the strength that women have. They encourage us in our callings and support us in the process. We aren't substandard to them but equals. Sadly, there are also many individuals who have belittled women and reduced us to second-class citizens, here only to serve them. Even sadder, there are those who have used Scripture to manipulate the system and support their own ideas.

One verse that has been misconstrued is found in 1 Peter. This letter was written to believers who are labeled as "exiles," likely living away from their homelands during a time of great persecution against the early church. Peter writes to encourage them to continue living holy lives—a life set apart and different from what was considered the norm at that time. The goal was to live honorably so that those who did not know God would see the difference in their lives and desire to know more—just as we are called to live with different standards than those who are not followers of Jesus. Peter calls on them to honor people around them no matter how they are acting.

By the time we get to chapter three, it starts with, "In the same way…" It's as clear as drawing an arrow and noting it with "see above." But some have taken the direction given to wives here to mean you have to be subservient to your husband. He has the right to rule with an iron fist and you must be meek and helpless, doing whatever he desires because he is over you. No! Submitting to your husband is equivalent to honoring and respecting him. Lift him up. Encourage him. Pray for him. Men crave respect. We as wives hold the very delicate ego of our husbands in our hands. They will rise to meet the acclaim we create for them, but they are just as likely to succumb to nothing more if all we do is nag and complain to and about them. We set the standard. We set the expectations. If we treat our husbands honorably, they will act honorably in return. It may not happen overnight, but there is tremendous power in the prayers of a wife for her husband. This same mindset takes us into verse seven of the third chapter of First Peter.

"Husbands, in the same way, live with your wives in an understanding way, as with a weaker partner, showing them honor as coheirs of the grace of life, so that your prayers will not be hindered" (1 Peter 3:7, CSB).

I personally don't like being called weak. I don't appreciate it when a man comes along and assumes I am incapable of doing something simply because I am a woman. I work hard to strengthen my body—mostly to be healthy—but I also won't deny that my husband is in fact stronger than me. It's not an insult; it's biology. Men are created with different hormones that allow them to develop muscles differently than women. Different does not mean better or worse, it's simply different.

Think about a clay pot. I have a small terra cotta pot that sits outside my back door. My middle daughter grew a bean sprout at school to learn about the different growth stages in plants and had lovingly asked if we could keep her "beanstalk." It was a lima bean and I have a notoriously black thumb, so I wasn't looking to invest a whole lot but still wanted to accommodate her. So, we bought the little pot for probably around $1 and replanted her beanstalk. Unfortunately, this was right before we left for a two-week trip in the middle of the Texas summer so needless to say, the little plant didn't make it long.

I unceremoniously dumped the pot out and have left it sitting on my back porch ever since. Eventually, I'll get around to planting a little flower or something in it, but in the meantime, I'm not too worried about it, knowing that that pot's purpose is still intact and ready for whenever I want to utilize it.

Now let's think about fine china. In January of 2020, my husband was able to work out the details for me to join him for a week of his three-week long work trip to Japan. He has been there numerous times, but this was my first time to experience this beautiful country. While he was at work, I had the not-so-tedious task of wandering and exploring the city of Nagoya. In my wanderings, I found a garden that was created around the foundation of an old ceramics plant. This garden, while beautiful despite the lack of color due to the winter season, was just the precursor as I continued to find a museum depicting the intricate process of creating bone china. Amazed at the beauty and in want of a souvenir, I purchased two small china teacups.

It may seem obvious but one of the materials used in bone china is in fact bone (typically bovine). Unlike other materials, it is fragile and precious. But being more fragile doesn't make it any less useful. How I treat something made from dirt (like my pot) is vastly different than how I treat something made from bone (like my teacups). Neither can take the place of the other and both are meant to be filled and utilized. Genesis 2 tells us that man was formed from the dirt of the earth. He's built to be sturdy. Woman was crafted from a rib bone. She's not less useful but is in fact created differently.

This verse in 1 Peter isn't meant to insult women as weaker of mind or spirit. It even addresses the fact that we are co-heirs! It is meant to remind husbands that their wives are precious vessels. Not helpless, precious. He is called to protect her and care for her not because she can't take care of herself, but because she is valuable.

Ladies, we have been in a fight from the very beginning. Genesis 3 tells us the story of the serpent who deceived. Unfortunately, both Adam and Eve succumbed and fell to the temptation. Because of that there were consequences, but I find it so poignant that when God addresses the serpent, He tells him that there will be enmity between him and the woman. That word enmity isn't just a mild dislike. It isn't like your friend of a friend who you deal with only because you know that your close friend likes them, though you don't understand why. This isn't like how you just smile and nod, biting your tongue, among in-laws you don't particularly like or get along with. Enmity is a word of war. God says that there will be a full-out battle between the enemy and women and that hasn't changed to this day.

"So the Lord God said to the serpent: Because you have done this, you are cursed more than any livestock and more than any wild animal. You will move on your belly and eat dust all the days of your life. I will put hostility between you and the woman, and between your offspring and her offspring. He will strike your head, and you will strike his heel" (Genesis 3:14-15, CSB).

God was establishing the first Messianic prophecy—the first foretelling of what Jesus would do to save us—and the enemy went on the offensive. He attempted to undermine women to disrupt the seed that would eventually be the Christ. Today, he is still attacking. Just like I said earlier, women are still giving birth to more than children. We are giving birth to truth, and promise, and hope, and the enemy is wanting to destroy that before it can come to fruition.

Sarah Jakes Roberts, a talented speaker also blessed with the gift of prophecy, created beautiful imagery when she talked about women today still being bitten by the enemy. She says that "The injury can be crippling but when we take a step forward, we are proving that it is not fatal."[3]

Ladies, as we step forward into the promises of God, we are crushing the skull of the enemy. We know that we aren't taking the place of what Jesus accomplished through his death on the cross and conquering the grave. He crushed the skull of the enemy to completion, taking back the authority that was stolen from us in the garden that day. But our steps forward crush the enemy's skull as we step into those promises accomplished on the cross. As we step out into our callings. As we step out into our passions. As we step out into who we are meant to be.

WE ARE WARRIORS.

The word ezer actually appears 21 times in the Old Testament. Two of those times are found in Genesis with the creation of woman.

Then the Lord God said, "It is not good for the man to be alone. I will make **a helper corresponding to him**." The Lord God formed out of the ground every wild animal and every bird of the sky, and brought each to the man to see what he would call it. And whatever the man called a living creature, that was its name. The man gave names to all the livestock, to the birds of the sky, and to every wild animal; but for the man **no helper was found corresponding to him**. So the Lord God caused a deep sleep to come over the man, and he slept. God took one of his ribs and closed the flesh at that place. Then the Lord God made the rib he had taken from the man

---

[3] Sarah Jakes Roberts. Bruised Heel Society.

into a woman and brought her to the man. And the man said:
This one, at last, is bone of my bone
and flesh of my flesh;
this one will be called "woman,"
for she was taken from man. (Genesis 2:18-23, CSB, *emphasis mine*)

The highlighted words are translated from the words *ezer kenegdo*. The Hebrew Lexicon Brown, Driver, and Briggs says it this way: "I will make him a help corresponding to him i.e., equal and adequate to himself."[4] It is two parts to one whole. Ezer is formed from the root word *azar*, which literally means to surround, protect, or aid. It is to support in times of hardship or distress.

Twenty-one times this word is used. We know the two that refer to the woman and for whatever reason, we've ignored how it's used everywhere else. We see a partial and inadequate translation as "helper" and assume that she is meant to serve in the supporting role to man. But how is it used the other nineteen times in scripture? Three times it is used to refer to needing military aid from a foreign country. I admit that I am not a military strategist, but in my humble opinion, I don't believe that when you are seeking military help from an allied nation that you would look to someone who is weaker or less qualified than yourself. If I'm being completely honest, when I am facing battles in my own life, I want the help and support of someone who is stronger than me. I want the strongest, most powerful, and most competent person in my corner doing battle with me.

It's important to note that the rest of the times ezer is used in scripture, it is used as a title for God. It is used to cry out to Him

---

[4] Brown, Driver, Briggs and Gesenius. "Hebrew Lexicon entry for `ezer". "The KJV Old Testament Hebrew Lexicon".

when the Israelites needed help. It was a name for God used when they were calling out for His support to surround them and to do battle for them. It was the cry for a mighty warrior.

Ezer kenegdo, while translated as "helper corresponding to him" can more accurately be translated as a warrior.

Ladies, we were created from the very beginning to battle and wage war. We may be created differently, but we are just as powerful and just as important. Our roles and purposes are not confined to being subservient to our brothers in Christ. In Matthew Henry's Commentary of Genesis 2, it says, "not made out of his head to rule over him, nor out of his feet to be trampled upon by him, but out of his side to be equal with him, under his arm to be protected, and near his heart to be beloved." While this is a beautiful picture, I have come to believe that it isn't always a complete understanding. In perfection, I believe this imagery can fit. But so often in this life, while the final battle has already been won, we are still actively fighting.

Ephesians 6 says:

For our struggle is not against flesh and blood, but against the rulers, against the authorities, against the cosmic powers of this darkness, against evil, spiritual forces in the heavens. For this reason take up the full armor of God, so that you may be able to resist in the evil day, and having prepared everything, to take your stand. Stand, therefore, with truth like a belt around your waist, righteousness like armor on your chest, and your feet sandaled with readiness for the gospel of peace. In every situation take up the shield of faith with which you can extinguish all the flaming arrows of the evil one. Take the helmet of salvation and the sword of the Spirit which is the word of God (Ephesians 6: 12-17, CSB).

We have both a shield and a breastplate to help guard our front, but that still leaves us vulnerable from behind. I love action movies that have strong character development. You see the protagonists grow closer and stronger until it culminates in that epic battle scene where back-to-back the heroes fight the enemy on all sides. One of my favorite fight scenes is from Marvel's *Endgame*. There are two parts of the last battle that stand out to me. *Spoiler Alert!* The first is when everyone first shows up. Captain America is nearly defeated and he knows it, but at the perfect moment, the interdimensional paths open and everyone, from all periods of time and distance, steps out and levels the playing field. The next part that stood out was toward the end of the battle. The men are spread thin and poor Spider Man realizes he's out of his league and in desperate need of help. That's when the women step up and take over getting him where he needs to go. They combine their focus and fight with as much skill and grit as every other Avenger on the battlefield. Even though it seems like they are surrounded and outmatched, they parry and strike in perfect unity—utilizing each other to battle effectively and efficiently.

That is the role of an ezer. That is who we are created to be. God didn't create a helper to sit back, but to stand up and wage war alongside her brothers and sisters in Christ. Together, watching each other's backs, holding each other up, we battle effectively and efficiently. This is how we become known as skull crushers.

CHAPTER TWO
BATTLE WORN

Warrior women is not a new, ultra-liberal, feminist idea. It was God's original idea at the creation of ezer. While the enemy has been busy launching attacks, finding different ways to marginalize women—and thus concealing the work God intended men and women to partner on together—women have still managed to slip into the patriarchal telling of history over the ages.

In each chapter we will look to different women in scripture to learn from the tools and characteristics God gave them to fulfill their roles as ezer-warriors. However, before we do that, I want to briefly dig into secular history to tell the stories of some of the literal warrior women throughout history and perhaps change our understanding of the narrative we've been taught. This is in no way meant to be complete—there are volumes of scholarly history books seeking to accomplish that. This is to serve as a clarification that this isn't a political agenda-driven idea, crafted to coerce greater support from a specific constituency. This is to serve as a place to show the inherent strength that lies within each and every woman around the world. The Biblical examples will show the scope of how we might battle differently, depending on the situation, but this brief look at history will support the idea that women have been going to battle for a myriad of reasons for an exceptionally long time.

The brief overviews will highlight several specific women and/or people groups, separated by different periods of history. These examples are not meant to automatically serve as role models beyond their strength and perseverance. Like all of us, they had their own faults and shortcomings that led some of them to choose less moral and honorable choices throughout their lives. But just as we learn from the mistakes and shortcomings of those in scripture, we can still see these women for what they accomplished and how they fought against what we have been told is the norm and expected of us as the "weaker sex." Their lack of decorum is part of the reason why we know they existed in the first place.

Laurel Thatcher Ulrich wrote, "Well-behaved women seldom make history." As a strong-willed woman, I find this idea percolating through my mind into my heart. No, I don't seek to inherently make history or be famous, but I—like so many—do want to leave a legacy of both strength and integrity. These women in history are remembered for scorning the societal expectations for women and stepping out in defiance.

According to those same societal norms, war is viewed as a man's world. Women are too delicate to deal with the brutal reality of battle, but when we begin to dig into history, we find women standing along with men to battle the enemy before them. Both biblically and anthropologically we find women who were fierce warriors, defending their homes, families, and beliefs.

Some of these women's names are readily recognized, like Joan of Arc, whereas entire cultures, like the Scythian warriors, are completely passed over in most history classes. We see the female warrior as the exception to the rule rather than the standard. A woman's place is set, and it doesn't involve battle, or so we've been led to believe. Instead of continuing the same narrative, let's see what roles women have actually played.

Ancient Warriors

One of the earliest records of a female military leader is that of Fu Hao. She lived during the Shang dynasty, one of the earliest ruling dynasties in recorded history, and was the consort of Emperor Wu Ding, who is traditionally recorded as ruling from 1324-1266 BC.[5] When their territory was threatened by a tribe to the north, Fu Hao volunteered to lead the military campaign. She had trained to fight when she was young and had recently traveled through the provinces alongside the emperor, allowing her to be well acquainted with the geography of their land. Recognizing her merit, the emperor granted her the commission. She led them to victory and later led three other successful campaigns against enemies attacking their territory.[6] Fu Hao was a general and queen consort but was not the exception. Archeological finds have discovered records of over 100 women's names listed as active in military campaigns during this same time.[7]

Thirteenth century BC China wasn't the only ancient civilization to have warrior women. Archeological digs in what is now Kazakhstan reveal a nomadic group from the 5th Century BC known as the Scythians. Are you familiar with the Greek mythology of the Amazons? If you happen to be drawing a blank, you could reference

---

[5] History.com Editors, "Shang Dynasty." (October 15, 2019). https://www.history.com/topics/ancient-china/shang-dynasty. Accessed 6/2/2020.

[6] "Fu Hao (fl. 1040 BCE)." Women in World History: A Biographical Encyclopedia. Encyclopedia.com. (May 23, 2020). https://www.encyclopedia.com/women/encyclopedias-almanacs-transcripts-and-maps/fu-hao-fl-1040-bce. Accessed 6/2/2020.

[7] Ibid.

either Homer (who called them the "equal of men") or the myths of the tribe of women who fought against Hercules. If your information references are a little less classical and a little more pop culture, you could also recall Wonder Woman. She was supposed to be an Amazonian. Those stories, obviously exaggerated to disproportionate heights, were still constructed from a kernel of truth. The stories developed from interactions the Greek travelers had with this tribe. It wasn't a group solely of women who abandoned their sons in favor of daughters, nor did they mutilate themselves to fight better as some inaccurate histories insinuate. Instead, the Scythian were known to raise their sons and daughters similarly—training both to shoot their specially crafted bows, hunt, and fight.[8] Traditionally, archeologists deemed any body found buried with weapons a male and a warrior. With the advancements in DNA analysis however, scientists were able to confirm that around a third of those Scythian bodies buried with weapons, while accurately confirmed to be warriors, were women.[9] They were respected warriors and thus received a warrior's burial just like the men.

Continuing westward, there was an ancient Celtic tribe that lived in what is now Portugal. In 138 BC Roman commander, Sextus Junius Brutus, was sent to subdue rebels in Lusitania and found "the women were 'fighting and dying with the men with such bravery that they did not cry out even when being slaughtered.'"[10] Greek historian, Appian, records that they fought fiercely, "never turning,

---

[8] Smithsonian Channel. "Epic Warrior Women: Amazons Episode 1." https://www.smithsonianchannel.com/shows/epic-warrior-women/amazons/1004515/3437447. Viewed 5/27/2020.

[9] Ibid.

[10] Chrystal, Paul. "Women at War in the Classical World." June 12, 2017. Pen and Sword Military.

never never turning their backs or uttering a cry."[11] Even to the ever patriarchal Roman society, these women were acknowledged and recorded for their ferocious bravery even unto a very gruesome death. Though, most women are likely not surprised to learn that these women would defend their families with such ferocity.

Sticking with Roman history, let's look at another group of fierce women who are generally not included in the history books. Gladiator games were initially developed as a part of funeral rites, acting out epic fights and scenes. Most modern (though not necessarily historically accurate) understandings of these games come from the money-driven mind of Hollywood, including the inevitable death at the completion of the battle. Unlike the movie depictions, not every battle ended in death. In fact, most gladiators were highly trained slaves who were incredibly valuable to their owners—even more so if they were able to continue to battle and win.

Ancient Rome was a male-controlled society and women had very few choices that they could make for themselves. They were defined and dictated to by their relationships to men, either as daughter, wife, or other relative. A woman's key roles and objectives were looking after the home and bearing children. Their reputation was either that of respectable or prostitute, with little to no middle ground. But there was another choice that they could take: choosing to become a gladiatrix.

Ancient texts refer to female gladiators as either a "ludia," for female performers, or as "mulieres," which simply refers to women. This might indicate that they were mainly lower-class as the word used for ladies, "feminae," was rarely used.[12] Just like their male

---

[11] Ibid

[12] Mark, Joshua J. "Female Gladiators in Ancient Rome." *Ancient History Encyclopedia.*

counterparts, female gladiators had a chance at fame and fortune, but it also gave them more independence despite giving up respectability. That independence proved to be a stronger incentive as laws were created to attempt at limiting this option.

A law passed by the Senate in the 11th Century AD forbade any woman under 20 and not born as a slave from participating in the gladiator games. In AD 200, Emperor Septemus Severus outlawed the participation of any woman. Possible motivation for this included the desire to prevent the female athletes from wanting to participate in the Olympic games, as well as blocking high-class women who might choose the gladiator games over marriage and life choices that were limited and dictated entirely by their male relatives.[13] Despite these obstacles, there is evidence that women were still fighting in the 3rd Century according to inscriptions found in a port city near Rome.

These women were specially and brutally trained. Their choice allowed them to enter the ring, entertain the masses, and despite the pugnacious nature of the job, there is evidence suggesting some of the female gladiators were actually the daughters of and trained by those fighters previously retired. No matter their reasoning, it is clear that they—along with so many others—were fierce warriors in the ancient world.

These four examples are marginal compared to the history that is now verifying the combative roles that women held in the ancient world. These women are from across the globe, in a multitude of different tribes and regions. Even the societies we might view as staunchly patriarchal to the point of treating women as little more

---

Last modified April 5, 2018. https://www.ancient.eu/article/35. Accessed 6/4/2020.

[13] Ibid.

than property to either their benefit or detriment have history that points to women stepping up and defending their own people, village, or family. While I'm personally against using Wikipedia as an actual reference (I double check any reference I find on there), I do suggest you perform a quick search for women in ancient warfare. You'll find a fairly lengthy list of names and places, spanning the centuries of time.

(NOT SO) COMMON ERA

Transitioning from the ancient world to the still really old but not quite ancient times brings us to more records of battle-worn women. Like the misconception of the Scythian burial sites, any Viking warriors' burial sites were previously assumed to be male. However, the researchers at Stockholm and Uppsala Universities used DNA analysis to confirm that a particularly famous burial site of a warrior found was a woman's. She was buried with several weapons indicating the warrior status as well as two horses and a full set of game pieces and board. These pieces "suggest that the person buried was a high-ranking combatant who was knowledgeable of strategies and tactics."[14] In other words, a brilliant military leader who was highly honored and respected for what she did.

Viking society was known to give women equal rights, though many scholars previously believed that their roles were still largely domestic. This idea is particularly interesting when paired with Norse mythology and literature, both of which depict strong women who take care of business. One of the most famous types of women from the sagas are the shieldmaidens—the mortal warrior version of the mythological Valkyries. Saxo Grammaticus describes them in

---

[14] Morgan, Thad. "DNA Suggests Viking Women Were Powerful Warriors." *History Channel News.* Last Modified March 5, 2019. http://www.history.com/news/dna-proves-viking-women-were-powerful-warriors.

his telling of the Battle of Bravalla, claiming 300 shieldmaidens fought for the Danes.[15] One such shieldmaiden, according to the same telling from Saxo Grammaticus, was Lagertha. The grandson of the slain Norwegian king, Ragnar, was seeking vengeance against the king of Sweden. On the way to exacting that vengeance, he was met at his camp by some of the shieldmaidens, dressed in men's attire and ready for battle. Lagertha was among them. Saxo describes her as, "a skilled amazon, who, though a maiden, had the courage of a man, and fought in front among the bravest with her hair loose over her shoulders. All marveled at her matchless deeds, for her locks flying down her back betrayed that she was a woman."[16] Legend or not, sagas tell of her victories as a fierce warrior.

For Western European women, the Middle Ages were largely dictated by the Church and the aristocracy. The thought was that everyone should stay in their proper place as established through a feudal government which classified every individual as either clergy, noble, or serf. While the clergy and nobility dominated the narrative, it is widely accepted that female serfs worked alongside the men as equals or near-equals. Women's rights in general continued to grow through the eras via the development of concepts relating to courtly love and chivalry. In addition to the realities that developed from the Black Death pandemic which killed so many that women were granted permission to take over their deceased husband's businesses.

Women in general were either demonized, as the church associated them with Eve and the fall of humanity, or they were under the

---

[15] Mark, Joshua J. "Ten Legendary Female Viking Warriors." *World History Encyclopedia.* Last modified January 9, 2019.
https://www.worldhistory.org/article/1300/ten-legendary-female-viking-warriors/.
Accessed 6/5/2020.

[16] Groeneveld. Emma. "Lagertha." *World History Encyclopedia.* Last modified November 2, 2018. https://www.worldhistory.org/Lagertha/. Accessed 6/5/2020.

expectation of perfection when compared to the Virgin Mary. Clergy at the time heavily relied on verses (out of context) to support the idea of men in authority over women to the point that women were little more than property to be used and traded however would best behoove the men and their financial and societal goals.[17]

Still, there were women who went against expectations. One such woman was the ever-popular Joan of Arc. Born to poor farmers in 1412, Joan was raised traditionally to be versed in domestic duties and to be exceptionally pious. She began having visions that she would be the savior of France, ensuring that the Dauphin, Charles VII, took the throne. In 1428, she cut her hair, dressed as a man, and ventured to Charles' court. When she successfully identified the Dauphin despite him being in disguise, she won herself an audience with him. She finally convinced them to allow her to accompany the army to Orleans where there was an English siege. The French won the battle and on July 18, 1429, Charles VII was crowned king of France.

The following spring, Joan was sent to battle a Burgundian assault. During the battle she fell off her horse and was captured. The Burgundians ransomed her to the British and she faced 70 different charges, including, but not limited to: witchcraft, heresy, and dressing like a man.[18] We all know the end of the story—she was found guilty (with no proof) and burned at the stake. It wasn't until 1456 that Charles VII finally spoke up for her, declaring her innocent of the charges and designating her as a martyr.

---

[17] Mark, Joshua J. "Women in the Middle Ages." *World History Encyclopedia.* Last modified March 18, 2019. https://www.worldhistory.org/article/1345/women-in-the-middle-ages/. Accessed 6/5/2020.

[18] https://www.biography.com/military-figure/joan-of-arc. Accessed 8/21/20.

Shifting our journey both around the world and throughout time, a little more than a century later, in what is now Nigeria, there was a warrior queen who fought ferociously to earn the same esteem as the male soldiers. Her name was Amina. Upon her father's death, her younger brother, Karama, took the throne while Amina continued training as a warrior. She was fierce and devoted throughout her training, ultimately winning the respect of the male-dominated military. When her brother died, she became the first queen of Zazzau. Only a few months after becoming queen, Amina led her soldiers into a military campaign. It is reported that she had 20,000 men under her command, and she ruthlessly led them in conquest after conquest.[19] These battles led to the expansion of their territory and increase in their wealth. She is also attributed to many military innovations including the building of fortified walls around the cities. Still today she is remembered as a fearless warrior queen who ruled for 34 years.[20]

NOT SO VERY LONG AGO

Queens and saints, even Gladiator games seem like stories we tell ourselves to encourage us to be stronger in the face of generic adversity. But there were women warriors in every region of the world, in every period since the dawn of time. They aren't the exceptions. They may have disguised themselves as men or became overly ruthless to even be accepted, but they were there. This is true for more recent battles as well.

In 1876, North America found itself at the mercy of westward expansion and caught in its crosshairs were the many tribes who called the west their home. It was typical for the men to be the

---

[19] https://www.bbc.com/news/av/world-africa-44888718. Accessed 8/21/20.

[20] "Queen Amina." World Eras. Encyclopedia.com. (August 11, 2020). https://www.encyclopedia.com/history/news-wires-white-papers-and-books/queen-amina. Accessed 8/21/20.

warriors who faced the soldiers, but one Cheyenne woman, named Buffalo Calf Road Woman, stepped up to battle against those who were advancing to take her village. Amid the battle, she spotted her brother trapped by soldiers. Without hesitation, she rode into the gully despite the flying bullets, and rescued her brother by pulling him onto her horse and riding to safety. In her honor, her people called her Brave Woman and named the battle after her: "The Battle Where the Girl Saved Her Brother."[21]

Only a week later she again battled against General Custer. While she and her people were victorious in that battle, only five months later the Cheyenne were attacked yet again and ultimately, they had to surrender and journey into foreign Indian Territory in what is now Oklahoma. Surrounded by unknown diseases, inhospitable land, and horrible conditions, Buffalo Calf Road Woman and 300 other Cheyenne were determined to return to their home. They managed to escape, and she was among those who defended her people throughout their journey home. While her story is sad, her determination is impossible to miss. She was respected as a warrior and remembered for the fierce defense of her people.[22]

Buffalo Calf Road Woman is one of many women throughout history who fought to defend their homes and their families. During the Civil War, women would serve as nurses treating the soldiers, but they also disguised themselves to fight for what they believed. During the World Wars, the typical image is that of women in the factories, braving the responsibility of taking on the "men's work," so the brave men could fight overseas. We don't often hear of women fighting, but there were some female battalions, like Maria

---

[21] Agonito, Rosemary. "Buffalo Calf Road, Heroic Cheyenne Warrior Woman." https://amazingwomeninhistory.com/buffalo-calf-road-cheyenne-warrior-woman/. Accessed 08/21/20

[22] Ibid.

Bochareva and the Battalion of Death from World War I. The same was true during World War II, including an incredible group of female pilots nicknamed the Night Witches.

This all-female unit of Soviet bombardiers was forced to fly in outdated crop-dusters that had been used for training, with no protection from the elements they flew through—neither the cold of the night air nor the bullets that were aimed their way. Their uniforms were male hand-me-downs, complete with oversized boots that did little to protect them from frostbite during their frigid flights. Not only were they working with hand-me-downs, but they had to do completely without some items that we would probably consider essential: parachutes, radars, guns, and radios.[23]

Despite the trials set against them, they dropped 23,000 tons of bombs on Nazi targets and were so feared that any Nazi that downed one of them was automatically awarded the illustrious Iron Cross. Their planes were so small that they were undetectable on radar, leaving their targets with only a slight whooshing sound as a warning of their coming demise. Their skill, ferocity, and undetectable nature is how they developed the name of the Night Witches.

The women faced tough opposition, but still managed to execute eight to eighteen missions a night. Their final flight, on May 4, 1945, took them within about 37 miles from Berlin. Only three days later, the Germans officially surrendered.[24] Despite being a clearly integral group of pilots, they were disbanded and not even invited to join in the victory parades.

---

[23] Holland, Brynn. "Meet the Night Witches, the Daring Female Pilots Who Bombed Nazis By Night." (06/07/2017, updated 06/07/2019). https://www.history.com/news/meet-the-night-witches-the-daring-female-pilots-who-bombed-nazis-by-night. Accessed: 12/18/20

[24] Ibid.

The story is similar across most countries. The United States had more than 12,000 women enlisted in the Navy and Marine Corps during World War I and about 400,000 served during World War II. However, it wasn't until 1948 that the United States recognized women as a permanent part of the armed services through the Women's Armed Services Integration Act.[25] Until then, it was expected that women should just return to their "duties" and remain at home without fully acknowledging the impact that they made through their service.

TODAY'S FRONT LINES

Even though women were finally allowed to enlist and serve in the U.S. military following the act in 1948, most of their roles were still limited to non-combative positions. It wasn't until 1994 that women were allowed to serve in all military positions except ground combat. It was another nineteen years (2013) before the ban on women in combat would be lifted entirely though it didn't go into effect until 2015. Since then women have served in every position, including successfully completing the training for the illustrious Army Rangers and Navy Seals.

You might be sitting there thinking, "Thanks for the history lesson I didn't ask for, but who cares? How does this affect me?" And I hear you—it is a bunch of history, but unless we recognize where we came from, we will continue to make the same mistakes over and over again—including in our spiritual walks. If we aren't willing to acknowledge the impact that women had anthropologically throughout world history, why would we recognize the impact that the women in scripture had? They appear to play such a minor role.

---

[25] CBC News Online. "Women in the military—international." 05/30/2006. http://web.archive.org/web/20110817105207/http://cbc.ca/news/background/military-international/. Accessed 12/18/20.

We hear sermon after sermon lauding the character of David or Paul. We hear the parallels brought between the roles of Abraham, Isaac, and Jacob. We learn about young leadership through Timothy and about perseverance through Job. Name after name, lesson after lesson, it all calls forth the main characters—all of whom appear to be male. So, what was the role of women in scripture? Are they in actuality secondary or have we just overlooked their vital roles throughout scripture?

Second Timothy 3:16-17 says, "All Scripture is breathed out by God and profitable for teaching, for reproof, for correction, and for training in righteousness, that the man of God may be complete, equipped for every good work." (ESV) Man in this verse is referring to Mankind—everyone. All scripture. Not just the popular stories. Not just the male characters we're so familiar with. Each and every individual in the Bible is there for a reason and God wants us to seek Him to understand that relevance. Like I said, I believe that God is calling His daughters to rise and battle against the enemy. Back-to-back, arms linked with both brothers and sisters in Christ, we can wage war against the schemes of the enemy. This battle that rages around us is not going to get any easier. It's not going to just go away. And even if every single man of God were to step up into their roles, fully becoming all that God has called them to be, it would still not be enough because it's only half of the church. Women assuming that battle is the man's job puts us at a disadvantage and while the war is already won through the blood of Christ and the power of the Spirit, there are still victories to claim for our families, our neighborhoods, our communities, and our world.

The women mentioned in this chapter fought physically against very visible and tangible enemies. While what they accomplished (and continue to accomplish in today's militaries) was in no way easy, sometimes I wish our battles were that direct. The enemy we fight slinks into the darkness of our hearts and minds. He pits us against one another so that it feels like we're fighting our neighbor or political adversary when in reality there is only one enemy, and he is not any one human. So how do we battle an enemy we can't see? How do we battle against something that continually slinks away, changing shape and motive as seamlessly as the tide receding and returning?

God has given us direction and lessons to learn. He's given us wisdom and discernment to hear His voice and read His word and faith to believe Him. The next women we are looking at will give us some practical tools to use in battle as well as clarify some of the innate characteristics that live inside each and every one of us as daughters of God. So take up your arms and press in—it's going to be good. Spend minutes in your comfy Jesus spot and take notes.

"IF WE AREN'T WILLING TO ACKNOWLEDGE THE IMPACT THAT WOMEN HAD ANTHROPOLOGICALLY THROUGHOUT WORLD HISTORY, WHY WOULD WE RECOGNIZE THE IMPACT THAT THE WOMEN IN SCRIPTURE HAD?"

CHAPTER THREE
FIGHT YOUR BATTLE
HULDAH | 2 KINGS 22

According to Jewish tradition, there were seven female prophets. One of those was named Huldah. She lived and prophesied the same time as other more known prophets like Jeremiah and Zephaniah. Honestly, when I first began my research, I didn't even recognize her name though I recognized the name of the king she advised. King Josiah became king of Judah at an incredibly early age and was one of the few who did in fact seek to honor God. But to fully understand Huldah's role, we need to first understand the full context of her story.

You can find Huldah's story in both 2 Kings 22:8-20 and 2 Chronicles 34:1-28. These are both histories, but like any historical telling, the perspective is dependent on the author. In this case, the books of Kings were written while the Israelites were still in captivity. Because of that, it makes sense that it would have a more intentional focus on showing the history to emphasize the trials that result because of sin. The author was currently living out part of the consequences of the choices made by those who came before him. While 1 and 2 Kings were written during the time of captivity, Chronicles was written after the Israelites began returning to

Jerusalem and the promised land. Just like Kings emphasizes the consequences of making sinful choices, it also makes sense because of their circumstances that the author of Chronicles would have a more redemptive emphasis. They are the same history, the same telling of the people and kings following Solomon, but Chronicles includes stories that emphasize God's heart to redeem His people. It presents the Israelites' history in such a way as to show how while there were consequences for sinful choices, God redeemed those who turned back to Him.

To understand the full context of Huldah and King Josiah's story, we also need to understand the environment they were living in. Going back several generations, we see King Josiah's great-grandfather, Hezekiah, was a man who "relied on the Lord God" (2 Kings 18:5, CSB). His legacy is one that calls him faithful to God and that "not one of the kings of Judah was like him before or after" (2 Kings 18:7, CSB). This legacy is important because the wickedness of the kings was a thermostat of the people. When the king honored God, the people's hearts were turned toward God. But when the king worshiped idols and false gods, the people's hearts turned to wickedness and debauchery. The Kingdom of Israel had split after Solomon into the kingdom of Israel and the kingdom of Judah. David's line continued through the kingdom of Judah. Unfortunately for the kingdom of Israel, they had more wicked kings than Godly and fell to foreign nations during the fourth year of King Hezekiah's rule over the kingdom of Judah.

Despite his God-honoring legacy, once Hezekiah died, his son Manasseh took over and did what was evil in the sight of the Lord. He turned completely away from how his father had led and instead practiced witchcraft and divination, even sacrificing one of his sons to a false god. Manasseh's son, Amon, likewise "served the idols his father served." He was so venomous that he was assassinated by servants of the kingdom. So, Amon's eight-year-old son, Josiah, was made king of Judah.

Thankfully for the kingdom of Judah, Josiah took after his great-grandfather and "did what was right in the LORD's sight and walked in all the ways of his ancestor David; he did not turn to the right or the left" (2 Kings 22:2, CSB). During the 18th year of his reign (at 26 if you're keeping track), Josiah was attempting to clear the rubble and repair the temple. It was during this that the high priest found a long-lost scroll. He passed it along to the court secretary who brought it and read it to Josiah. Upon hearing the words, Josiah was greatly distressed and immediately sent his top five advisors to seek God's word on his behalf.

This is where we first meet Huldah. At this point you might be wondering, where is the battle? There are plenty of actual, physical battles in scripture—this isn't one of them. Instead, Huldah teaches us about fighting the battle that is in front of us—whether physical, emotional, or spiritual. She utilizes several key characteristics to stand up and answer the call God gives her. Think about these characteristics like tools in your tool belt.

Whether it's because I'm a writer, or maybe it's just a quirk in my own unique personality, I love office supplies. I love when I get to open a fresh ream of paper—especially if it's a heavier stock like the 28-pound paper I use to print my kids' homeschool sheets. Or the simple joy found in that special moment when I write for the first time in a new notebook. But my favorites are all the different types of writing utensils. I love pens of all colors, chosen more by mood than anything else. But when I'm taking notes or researching, there's something about writing in standard pencil that I appreciate. While silly, these are just a few tools of my trade. My foundation is the laptop I type on, but at different times for different purposes, I will pull out one of these other tools and put them to work.

Remember Ephesians 6:11 tells us to "put on the full armor of God so that you can stand against the schemes of the devil" (CSB). That includes the belt of truth, the breastplate of righteousness, feet shod with the gospel of peace, the shield of faith, helmet of salvation, and the sword which is the word of God (verses 13-17). While these are the foundation to our spiritual armor, there are other things that God equips us with to be able to make our stand against the enemy.

WE HAVE INFLUENCE.

The first tool that we see in Huldah's story is influence. The job title, "influencer" is fairly new, but the concept has always been around. Marketing will look to utilize those people who have the power to influence people's thoughts and actions to push us toward a certain product or idea.

Think about commercials you've seen on television. While there are plenty that employ a stock model, the ones we recall are often those who instead feature a famous actor we recognize on sight. The idea is that because we "know" these actors, we're more likely to trust their advice. This isn't only true for television commercials. Since you are sitting here reading, let's look at book marketing as well.

Many popular books will be marketed with their reviews. At the front of the book, before you've even begun to read, you'll find a page or two of short reviews by other famous authors and influencers. They'll tell you how intriguing the story is. They'll laud praises on the author. They—as influencers for that arena—will utilize their power to help sway you into purchasing that book.

Even the church does it. Due to the digital and social media age we live in, a pastor's reach can go well beyond the pews that stretch before him (or her) on Sunday morning. I personally attend what is known as a mega-church. The church alone has multiple campuses, music records, and well over 30,000 members (actual members, not counting just general attendance). The influence of the pastor reaches well beyond those who choose to attend one of the four services each week. He also has multiple books, often appears on Christian television programs, and is invited to speak internationally. He is an influencer—someone with the power to direct the thoughts and actions of others. When he recommends a book, article, or program, people will go out and purchase that book immediately following the service. They willingly accept what he says and believe him to have their best interest in mind. Influencers have the power they do because we trust them.

Huldah was an influencer. Let's look at what we're told about her when she's introduced to us in scripture.

"So the priest Hilkiah, Ahikam, Achbor, Shaphan, and Asaiah went to the prophetess Huldah, wife of Shallum son of Tikvah, son of Harhas, keeper of the wardrobe. She lived in Jerusalem in the Second District. They spoke with her" (2 Kings 22:14, CSB).

In this one verse we learn several things: she was a prophetess, the wife of the keeper of the wardrobe, and that she lived in the Second District of Jerusalem. On their own, these seem like innocuous facts, irrelevant even. The introduction, however, is informing us who she was and why she was important. The fact that she was a prophetess is a little obvious in this instance so let's look at the next piece of information. She was the wife of the keeper of the wardrobe.

The job title "keeper of the wardrobe" is referred to several times in the Bible. It refers to keeping and maintaining the ceremonial robes of the priest or king. Given the importance of the robes, scholars have assumed that Shallum was likely a Levite, the family line of priests who traced their lineage back to Aaron, brother of Moses. While it doesn't indicate whether these were the robes of the priests or the robes of the king, either would lend itself to being an honored and trusted position. He would have close interaction with persons of power and thus need to be a man above reproach. As wife to such a man, Huldah would have been expected to also live above reproach.

The last piece of information we're given about Huldah is where she lived: The Second District of Jerusalem. Some translate this as the college. This area was thought to be a suburb and new portion of the city where many scholars of God's word would come together to discourse and learn from their teachers.

There are differing opinions when it comes to this piece of information. Some commentators say that this was merely designating where she lived. Others believe the location tells us that Huldah, especially as a prophetess, would have naturally been a part of the scholar community. Traditionally, there is a location walking into the temple that is called Huldah's Gate. From this prominent place, she would teach and prophesy to those who came to learn. She was said to be well-learned, able to read and write unlike some other well-known prophets of the day. No matter what frame of thought you find yourself, one thing is clear, Huldah was a woman of influence.

As image bearers of God, we too are called to be influencers. This isn't a call to set up an Insta account solely devoted to posting Bible verses or require everyone to ascertain a Master of Divinity. This isn't requiring us to all live a perfect, unattainable life, hiding every shortcoming we have. In fact, people often relate to us best in our weaknesses. This isn't about the title of influencer as much as living a life that continually points back to God.

When I first began volunteering in the church, my husband and I served with Student Ministries. We had been volunteering only a few months when we chaperoned our first retreat with them. At this point, I'm in my early twenties, recently married, only a couple years out of college, and had unrealistic expectations of what it looked like for students–especially high school boys–to respect me as a leader. During one of the games, some words were said that showed they didn't know how to respect me and that I didn't really know how to lead them. One of the other, well-established leaders pulled me aside and reminded me that my role was unique. Yes, they needed to learn to listen to those in positions of authority, but I needed to also understand that yelling at them wasn't going to accomplish that goal. Being a leader to them meant more than just pointing out when they were wrong or when trying to get them to do whatever I told them to do. It meant guiding their actions to point back to Christ rather than acting out. It meant showing them by example how we are called to honor each other–no matter what title or position someone holds. It meant not beating them over the head with my supposed authority but directing them gently to discover for themselves the benefits of doing it a different way.

We're going to fall short. In fact, the book of Romans assures us of this when Paul proclaims that "all fall short of the glory of God" (Romans 3:23, CSB). But we have a merciful Savior who reaches out His hand, pulls us back to our feet, and points us back to the right path. He said, "For God did not send his Son into the world to condemn the world, but to save the world through him" (John 3:17, CSB). It was embarrassing to be pulled aside by another leader and withstand correction, but it wasn't done to condemn me but to help me. She didn't berate my ignorance, but offered a better, more honoring option for me to learn. Because someone was willing to guide me through my mistakes, I was able to become a better and more effective leader in the future.

Do you remember Jesus' interaction with the woman caught in adultery found in John 8? Jesus was teaching at the Mount of Olives when the scribes and Pharisees brought a woman to stand before Him. Her crime? Caught in the act of adultery. According to

Levitical law, the punishment for such a crime is death. Of course, the law states that both the adulterer and the adulteress are supposed to face this punishment and we see no sign of the man anywhere in this passage. We don't know if it was a trap for the woman. We don't know if she was well known for this act or if this was a one-time act of passion and lack of restraint. We just don't know, but what we do know is that the Pharisees were out for blood. They wanted evidence against Jesus, and this seemed like the opportune way to establish it. They paraded this woman before Him, quoted scripture, and pointedly asked what He had to say about it. I imagine them sneering smugly, thinking that they surely trapped Him this time. The Law was clear.

While I imagine the boys club waiting haughtily for Jesus' response, I also imagine the woman. Scantily clothed, her arms wrapped around her chest as her long, dark, and disheveled hair fell forward, tears silently streaking through the dust that was kicked up on her face as she was dragged out and then thrown to the ground. Embarrassed and scared, anticipating that moment when a rock will be hurled at her, striking her, and slowly breaking her until her life is buried beneath each of those stones bearing the weight of the accusations against her.

Then I imagine Jesus. I imagine His slight annoyance of these same men attempting to hijack His teaching again, knowing the intent behind their interruption. But then I imagine Him barely listening to the accusations, instead looking intently at the woman thrust before Him. Compassion and heartbreak for her flood His vision as the maliciousness of the men surrounding her collides against her before a single rock is thrown her way. He wasn't looking at her sin so obviously on display, but at her heart, seeing how desperately the Father loves His daughter. Thinking through the best response, He crouched down and began to write in the dirt.

The Pharisees, annoyed that Jesus once again hasn't responded the way they thought, continue to harp on Him. Internally He prays to the Father, then speaking with the full authority that is His says, "The one without sin among you should be the first to throw a stone at her." Part of me imagines this said with the bubbling energy of an innovative idea, dripping with sarcasm, already assured of the end result. Another part of me imagines a reverent solemnity about His demeanor, saying it with great thought and wisdom, much like a judge issuing his verdict to the courtroom. Finished delivering His mandate, He again crouches to the ground, waiting—knowing.

The Pharisees are dumbfounded, looking from one to another, some already turning red with both anger and embarrassment. Slowly, starting with the oldest, they slink away from the scene. When the last one realizes no one is still standing there to accuse the woman, his face contorts in frustration as he stomps off to find the rest of his crew.

The woman, still standing there shaking, glancing up through her hair as each man walked away. Confused, she jerks her head around, still certain that someone is standing there, ready to hurl a stone at her. Spinning slowly, all she sees are the shocked faces of those who were there before the Pharisees showed up until Jesus stands and meets her eyes. Expecting accusation, she finds only compassion and warmth reaching around her and into the depths of her heart and soul. A warm hug of divine love envelops her as Jesus speaks to her.

"'Where are they? Has no one condemned you?'

'No one, Lord,' she answered.

'Neither do I condemn you,' said Jesus. 'Go, and from now on do not sin anymore'" (John 8:10-11, CSB).

The woman wasn't defined by that one moment. It wasn't the end of her story; it was only the beginning. Jesus acknowledged her sin but then told her to stop making those choices. Just as He did for her, He does for us. He looks us in the eye, looking not at what we've done but at who (whose) we are. He speaks to that place inside of us that knows we messed up, pulling us up and saying, "Go and sin no more." Even as influencers we are not defined by our mistakes, but what we do in light of them.

Each of us will have a different level of influence—none better nor worse than the other. Jeremiah was a prophet at the same time as Huldah. Most people automatically recognize His name, readily quoting the words he prophesied, while not even knowing Huldah's name. There are those who report that Jeremiah was illiterate so there was a scribe that worked alongside him to write down his words. Huldah's words weren't recorded in that manner. In today's standards, Huldah wouldn't have a large platform. She wouldn't have as many followers on social media nor have her quotes shared across the web. She might not be invited to speak at conferences around the globe or have a major book deal. But scholars agree that the finding and verification of the scroll (by Huldah) was the most important accomplishment of Josiah's rule.

The size of your following does not dictate the importance of your influence.

WE HAVE AUTHORITY.

The difference between influence and authority is that while influence is power, authority is the right to use that power. Huldah was an established prophet at the time the king's officials showed up at her door. This wasn't her first encounter nor some random happenstance. Verse 14 states, "So the priest Hilkiah, Ahikam, Achbor, Shaphan, and Asaiah went to the prophetess Huldah, wife of Shallum son of Tikvah, son of Harhas, keeper of the wardrobe. She lived in Jerusalem in the Second District. They spoke with her."

Some commentaries will try to make excuses for why they went to a woman. They'll claim that Jeremiah must have been out of town. Zephaniah, who was also a prophet during Josiah's rule, might not have begun his ministry yet or that he was still too inexperienced to be the king's first choice. But none of that is what scripture says. It simply states that they were instructed to go and seek the word of the Lord and they went to Huldah. That tells me she was the first choice, not secondary or tertiary.

Another claim for why they might choose Huldah over another male prophet was for the very fact that she was a woman. The commentators who make this claim insist that if she was chosen it was because they were wanting a more empathetic response to the promised destruction spoken of in the scroll. When I read this, I couldn't decide if I should be offended or laugh. Frankly, it's ignorant to assume just because someone is a woman, they automatically have more empathy. Yes, women are created to nurture, but that doesn't directly translate to empathy. I'm a good example of this. According to Gallup StrengthFinder, there are 34 unique strengths that every person in the world possesses. Our top five to ten are where we function most naturally. They explain why we might react to certain situations a certain way or excel in specific areas. My top strength is strategic. It "enables you to sort through the clutter and find the best route."[26] Empathy is my 26th (out of 34). Some might label that more of a weakness than a strength, but the point is that just because I'm a woman does not mean that I am going to inherently anticipate the need and respond with just the right tone to help the situation. I may see the need that you don't realize is there amidst the clutter due to the strategic strength, but my response is likely to be blunt, not empathetic.

---

[26] Gallup, Inc. "Strategic summary." 2020. My.gallup.com. Accessed 5/19/2020.

Like I mentioned before, when I first began ministry, my husband and I volunteered with the student ministry at our church. During the five years we served there, I developed close relationships with many of the girls I worked with, some whom I'm still close with today as our relationships shifted from leader to friend. But many of the young men were intimidated by me. When my husband and I were moving, they sought to honor us with final memories and words of encouragement before we left. They had incredible memories to share with my husband. Kind words of his leadership and laughter at his goofy nature. When they turned to speak to me, there was an agreed upon comment that when they first met me, they were scared of me. They may have tried acting out in typical teenage rebellion initially but quickly learned not to cross me (according to their words). That was it. No reconciliation to that intimidation that was entirely unintentional on my part. No encouraging words of any leadership. Nothing. While I admit to being abrupt in some of my dealings with them early on as I learned how to settle into my role as leader, the only difference between me and some of the other female leaders was my no-holds-barred responses. The only difference between how I handled situations and some of the male leaders was that I was female. I handled situations directly and didn't see the need in softening my responses to them—just like some of the guys, but they were seen as good leaders whereas I was seen as scary and abrasive.

Years later, God helped me walk through the hurt this seemingly innocent send-off left in my heart. I was able to both forgive those young men, who honestly just didn't have the know-how of working alongside a strong-willed woman and forgive myself for hating a piece of how I was created. In those years, God continued to refine and soften my words and actions, so they came off as less abrasive, but I didn't become the stereotypical gentle-natured woman. This continues to be a fine balance in my life as gentleness is a gift of the Spirit, but I am also created to be a strong and decisive personality, hard-wired to speak truth bluntly. I have learned that gentleness does not equal passivity, nor does it require me to soften the truth when the truth needs to be heard in its full strength as Huldah did when she answered the men's query. If we continue in the verses, I believe that Huldah's first recorded response to the men eliminates this idea of being the empathetic choice.

She said to them, "This is what the Lord God of Israel says: Say to the man who sent you to me, 'This is what the Lord says: I am about to bring disaster on this place and on its inhabitants, fulfilling all the words of the book that the king of Judah has read, because they have abandoned me and burned incense to other gods in order to anger me with all the work of their hands. My wrath will be kindled against this place, and it will not be quenched'" (2 Kings 22:15-17, CSB).

There are two important pieces to her response here. First is how God addresses them. Verse 15 says, "Say to the man who sent you to me…" God knows it was the king but doesn't distinguish him as any more important than anyone else. It sets the tone for the response that follows as if to say, "you're not going to get special treatment just because you're the king."

The second piece is a little word that seems meaningless: *"said."* When I first began college, I was a journalism major. I loved to write so it seemed like a natural, realistic option for future careers. Unfortunately, my style of writing was not very conducive to the non-emotional tone my professor was requiring on every single assignment. I had to simply report the facts. When quoting individuals, I wasn't allowed to extrapolate or emphasize with more creative reporting verbs. Said was the only option. Not exclaimed. Not dismissed. Not proclaimed. I was reporting, not deducing. In the instance of verse 15, *"said"* doesn't convey the heart of the verb it is translated from. The original word is *'Âmar*. Unlike the straightforward generic nature we attribute to *"said,"* the word

"'Âmar" is more accurately understood as declare or command. Huldah isn't merely speaking to these men; she is authoritatively canonizing the scroll they found and serving as the trusted mouthpiece for God.

Second Timothy 3:16-17 says, "All Scripture is inspired by God and is useful to teach us what is true and to make us realize what is wrong in our lives. It corrects us when we are wrong and teaches us to do what is right. God uses it to prepare and equip his people to do every good work" (NLT). Huldah is taking the words on the scroll, explaining what is written, and teaching them how God is using it to prepare and equip them. She is standing in the authority given to her by God and using that authority to battle the fear and despair the king felt upon hearing the initial judgment.

We too have been given authority.

Luke 10:19 says, "Look, I have given you the authority to trample on snakes and scorpions and over all the power of the enemy; nothing at all will harm you" (CSB)[27].

Hebrews 1:1-2 says, "Long ago God spoke to our ancestors by the prophets at different times and in different ways. In these last days, he has spoken to us by his Son. God has appointed him heir of all things and made the universe through him."

Official prophets (or prophetesses) were necessary before because the veil still separated us from being able to approach God directly. Priests had to offer the sacrifices for forgiveness, prophets were God's voice to His people. Then Jesus came and through His death on the cross, He tore the veil and opened the way for the Holy Spirit

---

[27] If you've never done a word study before, the Bible utilizes certain words to reference different things. In this case, snakes and scorpions allude to demons and the power of the enemy.

to come and fill every believer. We have a direct line to God so we can hear His voice for ourselves, and through the power of the Holy Spirit we are able to stand up in the authority given to us and battle anything that comes against us.

WE ARE ENCOURAGERS.

Influencers with God-given authority sounds pretty great, doesn't it? However, if we were to approach these with selfish ambition, what was given as a blessing would become our downfall. It's important to remember that these tools aren't given to us for our own power and personal gain. There are plenty of examples of God-loving individuals who allowed their pride to get in the way of what God was doing, making it all about themselves rather than the power of God, and ultimately it led to their ruin. We may not see it while still on earth, but we will ultimately be held accountable for how we utilized (or squandered) God's gifts. This power to direct the thoughts and actions of others (influence) and the right to do so (authority) ultimately exist so that we can encourage and empower others.

First Thessalonians 5:11 says, "Therefore encourage one another and build each other up as you are already doing" (CSB). Any skill or knowledge or advantage we might have is all to glorify God and to raise up those around us. Jesus reminded us that the greatest commandment was to "Love the Lord your God with all your heart, with all your soul, and with all your mind" (Matthew 23:37, CSB). But He continued on saying, "The second is like it: Love your neighbor as yourself. All the Law and the Prophets depend on these two commands" (Matthew 23:39-40, CSB). To love God is to love His creation—each other. Part of loving one another is encouraging one another.

Huldah played a monumental role in Biblical history by canonizing the portion of scripture found in the rubble of the temple. Her words confirmed that, yes, it was in fact the inspired word of God meant to teach us and to guide us. Scripture is used to teach, train, and encourage us.

Each one of us is to please his neighbor for his good, to build him up. For even Christ did not please himself. On the contrary, as it is written, **The insults of those who insult you have fallen on me**. *For whatever was written in the past was written for our instruction, so that we may have hope through endurance and through the encouragement from the Scriptures.* Now may the God who gives endurance and encouragement grant you to live in harmony with one another, according to Christ Jesus (Romans 15:2-5, CSB, *emphasis mine*).

The verses telling us about Huldah do not initially appear to be battle-ridden. There isn't an all-out war or spiritual attack. There isn't the clashing of swords but instead we find spiritual blows against the enemy as Huldah stands firm in speaking truth coupled with encouragement. Speaking truth—especially when that truth is difficult or not particularly what we want to hear—is an offensive attack against the enemy. He wants us down and out. Apathetic and disinterested. The enemy does not want us to speak truth and he certainly doesn't want us to build one another up. When we do these two things in tandem, we are equipping others to then stand up strong and firm in the authority given to them by God and do the same for others around them. It's a massive ripple effect that turns the tides of this war in favor of the Kingdom of God. The enemy is less concerned about whether or not we believe in God; he wants to make us ineffective.

When we figure out how to relinquish the power our sinful natures seem to crave and instead rest in confident assurance of the influence and authority given to us by God, speaking truth in love to build up those around us, lives are changed, war is waged, and battles are won for the Kingdom of God.

CHAPTER FOUR
WHAT DO I
HAVE TO GIVE?
JOANNA | LUKE 8 & 23

_____

While they aren't mentioned very often, history informs us that there were women among the followers of Jesus. We're very familiar with His twelve disciples, but often miss the fact that there were others who traveled from city to city with Him. Most remain unnamed, but there were three women specifically named in Luke 8.

Afterward he was traveling from one town and village to another, preaching and telling the good news of the kingdom of God. The Twelve were with him, and also some women who had been healed of evil spirits and sicknesses: Mary, called Magdalene (seven demons had come out of her); Joanna the wife of Chuza, Herod's steward; Susanna; and many others who were supporting them from their possessions (Luke 8:1-3, CSB).

While all three women could prove an interesting study, we're going to look specifically at Joanna. Before we do that though, we must look back to what was said just before this verse. Chapter eight, verse one begins with "afterward." Anytime scripture uses conjunctions to start a verse or chapter, like afterward, we need to look back to what was said before. It is telling us that whatever happened just prior is somehow important to what is about to happen.

In this instance, the story that ends chapter seven is the telling of the sinful woman who poured out an alabaster jar of perfume on the feet of Jesus as an offering. Jesus' response to her extravagance gives us a clue to how he will welcome us. She knew her sins were great, but she offered what she had in true repentance. Jesus welcomed her, loved her, and forgave her. He had already healed the centurion's servant, raised the widow's son, assured John of His identity, and called out the unresponsiveness of their generation. He hasn't been idle or exclusive. If anything, He continued to show that He came for all—not just the men of Jewish heritage.

Jesus welcomed the woman's offering, just as He continues to welcome each of us today. He wants us to come and bow at His feet with our doubts and fears. He wants us to pour out our insecurities and judgments. He wants us to come humbly but confidently, laying it all before Him as an offering. He can handle our big emotions and our big passions. He wants us to bring all that we are—the too much, too loud, too opinionated, too abrasive, too delicate, too weak, too girly, too butch, too big, too small, too whatever we've been labeled with—and worship Him fully.

The woman sought Jesus out, offered willingly, and in turn received the loving forgiveness of her Savior.

BE BOLD.

Directly following that story, we are introduced to a few of the women who walked with Jesus. Like I said before, we're going to look and learn from Joanna. All we know from scripture is that she was healed by Jesus (of demons or disease, it doesn't specify) and was the wife to Chuza, Herod's steward. Some translate her husband's position as the manager of Herod Antipas' household. In today's comparison, it would be like the chief financial officer.

This tells us a couple things. One, she would have lived in a much different social circle from that of Jesus. Her husband had an especially significant role in managing Herod's affairs so she would have likely lived in—or near—the palace and would have been fairly well-off. The main point being that Joanna would not have crossed paths with Jesus naturally or just by happenstance.

This particular Herod was Herod Antipas or Herod the Tetrarch. His father, Herod the Great, was the one who renovated the second temple in Jerusalem but was also responsible for the massacre of children at the time of Jesus' birth. The current Herod—Herod Antipas—was curious about John the Baptist's teachings and likely spoke about them within the walls of the palace. Joanna, as Chuza's wife, might have heard the talk about John and then also about this other prophet named Jesus. She might have heard that He was traveling around healing the sick and even raising the dead.

At the end of John 4, we find Jesus returning to Galilee after spending a few days in Samaria. Verse 46-47 says, "There was a certain royal official whose son was ill at Capernaum. When this man heard that Jesus had come from Judea into Galilee, he went to him and pleaded with him to come down and heal his son, since he was about to die." The people of Galilee wanted to see more signs and wonders, but this royal official—whoever he was—just wanted to save his son and believed that Jesus could do it. Jesus responded to his pleading, telling him his son would live, and the official departed. On the way, servants came and informed him that his son was alive and well. Upon hearing the time that he was healed—the exact time Jesus spoke that his son would live—the royal official believed on a whole different level. It transitions from "he believed" in verse 50 to "he himself believed" in verse 53. Upon experiencing the power of Jesus, the royal official didn't simply believe Jesus could perform some miraculous tricks. He had an encounter with the Messiah and believed completely in who He was. Not only did this change the life of the royal official (and obviously the son who was healed), but it says that his entire household also believed.

One of the similarities that we see each time Jesus performs a miracle or reveals himself is that word spreads. Jesus just came from Samaria where He had an encounter with the woman at the well. Once He revealed Himself as the long-awaited Messiah, she "left her jar, went into town, and told the people" (John 4:28 CSB). She saw, she believed, she went and told, and others believed "because of what the woman said when she testified" (John 4:39 CSB). I believe the same was true for this royal official. He saw Jesus, he believed, and then because of that his entire household also believed. Joanna, wife of Chuza, manager of Herod's household, likely could have interacted with this royal official or one of his household. The domino effect of one life changed through an encounter with Jesus leads to others around them being affected as well. Whatever her condition—either demon possession or infirmity—she might have thought to herself, "perhaps He could heal me too." So, she sought Him out.

Throughout scripture we find examples of God telling us if we seek Him, we will find Him. A well-known verse is found in Jeremiah 29:

"For I know the plans I have for you," declares the Lord, "plans to prosper you and not to harm you, plans to give you hope and a future. Then you will call on me and come and pray to me, and I will listen to you. You will seek me and find me when you seek me with all your heart. I will be found by you," declares the Lord (Jeremiah 29:11-14, NIV).

This verse was written by the prophet Jeremiah who was from the same time as Huldah, during the reign of King Josiah. We already learned that the Kingdom of Israel had fallen into the hands of invading kingdoms and the Kingdom of Judah was barely hanging on to its own sovereignty. God spoke through Jeremiah to tell of the coming judgment, but to also offer hope of redemption. Once the people of Israel humbled themselves and turned their hearts back to God, He would restore them. He had a plan already in place. He wasn't playing a vengeful game of hide-and-seek where the all-knowing God could keep Himself hidden for all time. Instead, He is like the dad who while playing hide-and-seek, hides under a couch pillow with his arms and legs both sticking out. The child only needs to turn and look, and they will immediately find him.

Jesus echoed this sentiment in Matthew when He said, "Ask, and it will be given to you. Seek, and you will find. Knock, and the door will be opened to you. For everyone who asks receives, and the one who seeks finds, and to the one who knocks, the door will be opened" (Matthew 7:7-8, CSB). The Bible assures us that if we ask, with pure motivations and our heart aligned with His will, He will answer us (Psalms 37:4-5).

For me personally, I typically find it easier to come to God with a need over a want. I'll sometimes try to justify the wants, but I still feel guilty because I know it's not a necessity. What I'm learning though is that if I am functioning from God's will, He doesn't mind us coming with the wants as well. Let me give you two examples of what I mean.

In August of 2016, my three children and I were in a serious car crash. Someone ran the red light and t-boned our car. My oldest, who was five at the time, sustained the most serious injuries in the form of an atlanto-occipital dislocation—or commonly known as an internal decapitation, as well as additional fractures to her C6 and

C7 vertebrae and extensive damage to the tendons and ligaments in her neck. She was unconscious at the scene and remained in the hospital for ten days following an emergency surgery to place her in a halo vest to stabilize her painfully fragile neck. Needless to say, our "need" list was long. We didn't know if she would suffer from paralysis or if she would regain full mobility. We didn't know if there would be additional surgeries, though we were warned by her neurosurgeon that more were very likely. We didn't really know what our life would look like from day to day to meet the new and ever-changing needs of our little girl. And that was only the beginning. Once we left the hospital, we discovered that we needed a specific vehicle to be able to transport her safely while she was in the halo. We needed finances to cover medical bills and for the insurance companies to step up and fulfill the coverage they promised. I was suffering emotionally following the accident, so my husband was needing to figure out how to continue providing for us financially, spiritually, and now even more emotionally to support me.

During a time of prayer, he came to God overwhelmed. Burdened and confused, trying to sort through insurance, legal-ese, and an anxiety-ridden wife, he sought after God. He cried out for God to meet our needs and in that moment, he found God. God spoke four words to him, "I am your provision." That was it. But what happened over the following year proved it to be the only four words we needed. God provided the van we needed, the support from family and friends to care for and love on us, complete miraculous healing of our daughter's bones, and even complete resolution with the insurance claims. In fact, the judge presiding over the case said that never before in her twenty years of law had she seen two insurance companies so completely come together and simply do what was in the best interest of the child. God was our provision. When my husband sought Him, He was found.

But like I said before, it's about more than simply what we need. Sometimes we need to be bold in asking for those things we want. When my husband and I first decided to buy a house, we began the journey of sorting through our wish list. We had always rented up to that point and knew that this wasn't meant to be the ultimate dream house, but something that we could use and grow as our family grew up.

Our realtor took us to see a number of houses, but ultimately, we felt that we wanted some of the structural assurances and warranties that could only be found in a new build. She brought us to an area that she knew had the neighborhood we wanted, closer to my husband's office, and closer to amenities. We looked at all the available floor plans and took home all the information and pamphlets.

That night, I sat on the couch after the kids were in bed, looking over each floor plan. I was imagining where I would place furniture, how we could utilize a particular space, and just trying to envision my family living in that space. There were several options that were easily within our budget, but I had already fallen in love with the layout that, while not beyond our budget, was at the very top of what we felt comfortable spending. Feeling somewhat defeated, I laid my head back and closed my eyes.

In that moment, God gently nudged me and asked, "What do you want?"

"I really want this one God," I responded, looking back over the pamphlet of that plan, already picturing our family making that house a home.

"Then just ask."

That was it. He was willing to support and bless us with the house I wanted; all I had to do was ask.

Joanna, despite her status, sought healing from this Jewish Rabbi she'd heard gossiped about throughout the palace. Instead of simply finding respite from her ailment, she also found her Savior.

GIVE GENEROUSLY.

Besides her marital status and her healing, the only other piece of information given about Joanna is that she and the other women listed supported Jesus from their possessions. We don't know if this was family wealth or perhaps, she received a stipend from Chuza to spend however she wanted. What we do know is that Joanna and these other women balked at societal norms by accompanying Jesus and His other followers unchaperoned and actively learning at the feet of their Rabbi—a place typically reserved for the male students of the teacher.

Joanna gave not only financially, but she gave up her status to follow Jesus throughout His ministry. This wasn't payment for her healing or a demand of any kind. This was, as scripture says, from the overflow of her heart. Second Corinthians 9:7 says, "Each person should do as he has decided in his heart—not reluctantly or out of compulsion, since God loves a cheerful giver" (CSB). Proverbs says it this way, "When it is in your power, don't withhold good from the one to whom it belongs" (Proverbs 3:27, CSB).

We are all instructed to tithe. This isn't that. This is the above and beyond. This is sharing our time and talents, and yes, sometimes our money as well if that's how we've been blessed and how God guides us to give. It can be determined by asking ourselves, "How has God blessed me right now?" It may shift and change in different seasons of life, but where are we in this moment and what blessings do we have to overflow on to others around us?

The novel coronavirus (COVID-19) pandemic was quite the experience. One day we were listening to reports out of China that they were beginning to establish quarantines, another day we're told to just wash our hands more diligently and treat it like we do any other virus. Then reports began popping up within the United States and everyone freaked out. No one knew what information was accurate and what was media hype. We watched as maps of the world showed hot spots of infection showing up here and there, appearing to spread at an alarming rate. So, in the interest of "flattening the curve" and "slowing the spread," we were placed in quarantine at the discretion of our government. Ordinances were issued to close non-essential businesses and life as we knew it changed.

My birthday is the second week of March. In Texas, we were monitoring the news but at that point everything was just covered in a banner of caution. I remember the morning starting horribly. The kids weren't getting along, there was a mess everywhere, and I just needed to get out of the house. This was the end of spring break and we all needed a break from each other. Don't worry, the irony isn't lost on me. We headed to the gym so I could sweat out as much frustration as possible and we headed home, still wound up and disappointed. When my husband called offering to bring me a special lunch, I essentially begged to meet up with him. The weather was gloomy and rainy, who knew if the children would cooperate, but all I knew is that I needed to stay out and about as much as possible. That evening we were gifted babysitting, so we went out again. After buying much-needed new running shoes, perusing Half-Price Books for an hour or so (walking out with several mindless, fun reads), we headed to dinner. It was a conflicting day overall as I remember the frustration, but also the fun and laughter with my gracious husband. There was a weird air around everyone, like we were all waiting for the other shoe to drop. Crowds were light as everyone was beginning to build their uncertainty. Then the news came that students would not be returning to school the following week. More businesses closed and we were quarantined to our homes for an unknown amount of time.

Y'all, I don't shy away from the reality that I'm an introvert. I hide it pretty well when I'm speaking or leading groups, but when all is said and done, I retreat to my spot on the couch, by myself with a good book. It's how I recharge. I love my people, but I certainly don't mind being home—usually.

The reality that became life during COVID-19 was, for lack of a better word, weird. It was weird not being allowed to see anyone. It was weird to just stay in the house, even though that was traditionally my retreat and safe space. It was weird to be wary of getting groceries and not being able to purchase even basic necessities because fear had prompted the masses to over-buy beyond what they needed even to constitute stocking up (something I'm intimately familiar with thanks to my years of living through hurricane seasons in Florida). It was weird to feel threatened by something that you couldn't see, knowing minimal information about it and even that was clouded with suspicion that there might be a conspiracy embedded somewhere within this crazy mass of ever-changing data. Like I said, it was just weird.

Where I felt it the most was not in the day to day or even in adapting to schooling my kids at home. It was on Saturday nights, when we would typically be going to church. As I've said, we go to a large church so there were certainly weekends when I could walk in and out without intentionally talking to anyone. More often though, I would be able to make connections with people I might not have seen any other time that week. I would touch base with women I served alongside, hug the necks of friends who had been sequestered by busy schedules or sick children, worship with fellow brothers and sisters in Christ—unified in that even if I didn't personally know their names or stories. Coming together in worship and hearing the Word of God preached ministered to my soul more than I realized. Yes, because of the resources our church has, we were able to watch service online every week without a hiccup. But there is something different about worshiping together in person. I began to understand why the author of Hebrews exhorted us saying, "And let us watch out for one another to provoke love and good works, not neglecting to gather together, as some are in the habit of doing, but encouraging each other, and all the more as you see the day approaching" (Hebrews 10:24-25, CSB).

Despite all the uncertainty and fear in that season, I began to see people stepping out and becoming the hands and feet of Christ. Our church has a text line that is available as a resource, but during this time it became a lifeline. If someone was laid off and unable to pay for their groceries, they could reach out and one of the pastors was able to approve funds to purchase groceries for that family. In need of activities and wanting to reach those who would be most lonely, families began tasking their kids with writing letters to be delivered to nursing homes, reminding those confined to their rooms that they weren't forgotten. We, like so many others, went on a baking spree, whipping up dozens of cookies, banana breads, and cakes. Goodness knows we couldn't (shouldn't) eat all of it ourselves, so we chose a few neighbors to bless with a card and giant bag of sugary goodness.

No matter the season, there is always something you can do. If you are blessed financially and can help fund children around the world, then do it. If you're blessed with wisdom and a heart to mentor, join the mentoring team at your church or local school and do that. If you have a heart for a particular group, find out what they need and serve how you're able. If you only have a limited capacity and time, use what you've got! Joanna was not only one of the financial supporters for Jesus' ministry but gave her time and position to follow Him. She took the provision she had been given and poured it back out in whatever way she could. We have been blessed to overflow. We were never meant to hoard the blessings from God, but to invest them and see them multiply so we can bless others around us.

DECLARE DECISIVELY.

God has given us not only hands and feet to serve, but a mouth to speak and declare. We are called to speak out with authority. We are called to tell others the good news of what Jesus has done for us! Joanna shows us this truth the next time that we see her mentioned at the very tail end of Jesus' earthly ministry. Luke 23:55-24:10 says,

The women who had come with him from Galilee followed along and observed the tomb and how his body was placed. Then they returned and prepared spices and perfumes. And they rested on the Sabbath according to the commandment.

On the first day of the week, very early in the morning, they came to the tomb, bringing the spices they had prepared. They found the stone rolled away from the tomb. They went in but did not find the body of the Lord Jesus. While they were perplexed about this, suddenly two men stood by them in dazzling clothes. So the women were terrified and bowed down to the ground.

"Why are you looking for the living among the dead?" asked the men. "He is not here, but he has risen! Remember how he spoke to you when he was still in Galilee, saying, 'It is necessary that the Son of Man be betrayed into the hands of sinful men, be crucified, and rise on the third day'?" And they remembered his words.

Returning from the tomb, they reported all these things to the Eleven and to all the rest. Mary Magdalene, Joanna, Mary the mother of James, and the other women with them were telling the apostles these things.

Luke tells it so succinctly, but Matthew's telling says that the ladies "departed quickly" from the tomb to go tell the disciples. I personally imagine them hiking up their dresses and running as fast as they could. Abandoning all sense of needed propriety, they had the ultimate news to share and wanted to do so as quickly as possible.

We see Joanna specifically mentioned two times in Luke's gospel. Once was at the beginning of Jesus' ministry and once at the end. Both times she sought after Him and both times He met her there. Each specific encounter left her with an experience to share with others. Joanna wasn't the only one who was ready to share after her encounter with Jesus.

Like I mentioned earlier, John 4 tells us about the woman at the well. Following her conversation with Jesus, John tells us that, "*Then the woman left her water jar, went into town, and told the people,* 'Come, see a man who told me everything I ever did. Could this be the Messiah?'" (John 4:28-29, CSB, *emphasis mine*).

There was also the man healed of leprosy, found in Luke 5. After Jesus healed him, He told him to present himself to the priests so he would no longer be considered unclean, but to tell no one else. I love that scripture tells us that the opposite happened instead.

While he was in one of the towns, a man was there who had leprosy all over him. He saw Jesus, fell facedown, and begged him, "Lord, if you are willing, you can make me clean."

Reaching out his hand, Jesus touched him, saying, "I am willing; be made clean," and immediately the leprosy left him. Then he ordered him to tell no one: "But go and show yourself to the priest, and offer what Moses commanded for your cleansing as a testimony to them. " *But the news about him spread even more*" (Luke 5:12-15, CSB, *emphasis mine*).

When we encounter Jesus, we can't not talk about it!

I think one of my favorite stories, however, is found in Mark 5. The story is a continuation from the previous chapter. Jesus had been teaching in parables to his followers then at the end of the day he tells them, "Let's cross over to the other side of the sea" (Mark 4:35, CSB). What may be missed in this simple exchange is that the parables he was teaching that day were all about planting and harvesting seeds—which represent the truth of the Gospel. It was about sharing with others in faith and recognizing that when that seed of truth took root, it would multiply greatly. The truth of God's love and the redemption through Jesus Christ is something that should spread to all who have ears to hear. From these lessons, Jesus had the disciples cross to the other side of the Sea of Galilee—during which time He demonstrated His authority over the wind and waves—to encounter a single man who had been cast out by society.

This man was possessed by not one, but an entire legion of demons (Mark 5:9-10). He couldn't control himself and was prone to fits of rage and insanity because of them. But upon seeing Jesus at a distance, even this legion of demons knew who He was. Jesus called out the evil spirits and sent them into a herd of pigs, who then proceeded to run over the bank and drown in the sea. When the people of the town came to see what happened, they found the man now sane and sitting dressed like any normal human being. Rather than rejoicing over the astonishing miracle, they were afraid and asked Jesus to leave. So, not being one to impose where He wasn't wanted, Jesus got back into the boat.

The man whom He rescued, however, begged to come with Jesus. Instead, Jesus told him, "Go home to your own people. And report to them how much the Lord has done for you and how he has had mercy on you." So he went out and began to proclaim in Decapolis how much Jesus has done for him, and they were all amazed (Mark 5:19-20, CSB).

WHAT DO I HAVE TO GIVE?

There were those who were scared and wanted nothing to do with Jesus and the mercy He offered, but the man had an encounter with Jesus and went to tell everyone how his life was forever changed. The Bible tells us that they were all amazed. Jesus crossed the sea, calmed a storm, and drove out a legion of demons to reach the heart of one man. But that one man then went to tell everyone he knew.

What message has God given you? What is your testimony? I used to feel intimidated by the idea of sharing my testimony. Not because I feared speaking to people, but because I didn't feel like I had much of a story to tell. I've learned that whether it's a physical or mental healing, the story of my salvation, or how God redeemed me from a false understanding, all our stories matter. It doesn't have to be a story of miraculous healing or a rags-to-riches experience. Sometimes, the most poignant stories are the everyday experiences, how God shows up in our everyday lives. How does He speak to us? How does He help us balance our stress and anxieties? How has He provided day in and day out, no matter what the outside circumstances may look like?

We battle through the stories we share. Rita Springer wrote in a devotional that, "We are not fighting *for* victory. We are fighting *from* victory." As we share our stories we are fighting against insecurities as it reminds us who has already given us victory. As we battle by sharing our stories, we encourage others around us to do the same—just as Joanna did when she shared the good news that Jesus had risen from the dead.

Go, declare what Jesus has done in your life, and know that you are actively waging war against an enemy who knows he has already been defeated by the blood of Christ.

"AS WE SHARE OUR STORIES WE ARE FIGHTING AGAINST INSECURITIES AS IT REMINDS US WHO HAS ALREADY GIVEN US VICTORY."

CHAPTER FIVE
CROSSING LINES
WITH CONFIDENCE
THE GENTILE MOTHER |
MATTHEW 15

Moms will do just about anything to help their babies. We use the terminology of "mama bears" because they will fight anything that they believe is a threat to their cubs. When I was in seventh grade, I had a teacher who, for whatever reason, turned down the project I submitted for the science fair. It met the requirements. It was turned in on time. I had even started some of the work for it since it was a continuation from my project the previous year (that won an award at the district level). The details around the teacher's response to me are a little fuzzy in my memory, but what is crystal clear is the interaction that followed.

My mom has always been a fierce mama bear. She is loving and protective of my sister and me. Still to this day, I believe she is willing to go to bat against anyone who might hurt us.

Following the rejection of my project proposal, my mom set up a meeting with my teacher. I wasn't privy to sitting in the room so I don't have a clue what was actually said. Instead, I waited out in the hallway, sitting against the lockers. What I do know is that I could hear them both, which indicates raised voices, and at the end of the conversation, I was allowed to proceed with my project as I had submitted it.

I, too, have told my kids that I will always fight for them if necessary. There's just something that stirs inside of me when it feels like one of my kids has been slighted. I'd probably lash out more often–with less effectiveness–if it weren't for my husband grounding me and ensuring I listen to the full story before going into beast mode.

Being a mama bear and doing whatever it takes to take care of your kids doesn't have to be an explosive interaction. It can be done in ways that show respect to the other person but doesn't back down from the fight. Even though I couldn't hear what was said, knowing my mom, I believe she showed respect to my teacher's position. I believe she acknowledged the challenges that come with being a middle school teacher but stood firm on the unfair treatment being shown toward me. This is part of our challenge. When we face battles, sometimes we aren't fighting something evil. Sometimes we have to stand up for what we know to be right, no matter what is said against us.

Learning from Joanna, we can begin to see how God might lead us into battle against the enemy. Her life and example are still able to guide us even though we don't have a record of any conversations she and Jesus had. Our next woman is someone who was never named but had her entire conversation recorded for all time. This exchange between a Gentile mother and Jesus can seem callous and insensitive upon initial reading, but if we understand both the heart of Jesus and the culture they lived in, we can find amazing direction for our own lives within this exchange.

The conversation is found in two places: Matthew 15 and Mark 7. It begins following the miraculous feeding of the five thousand, Jesus walking on the water (where Peter is asked, "Why did you doubt?"), and then the multitudes all bringing their sick to be healed. Matthew begins saying, "When Jesus left there, he withdrew to the area of Tyre and Sidon" (Matthew 15:21, CSB). Jesus left Jewish territory and went into an area where the Gentiles lived. He removed himself from those who knew who He was and who had seen and possibly experienced the miraculous. While this may have been an opportunity to take a short breather, it also sets the stage for Jesus to explain more of the purpose and plan and for us to understand that when we are called to battle, we will have to step beyond our natural comfort zones.

CRUSH COMFORT ZONES.

Matthew's telling continues saying, "Just then a Canaanite woman from that region came and kept crying out, 'Have mercy on me, Lord, Son of David! My daughter is severely tormented by a demon.'

Jesus did not say a word to her. His disciples approached him and urged him, 'Send her away because she's crying out after us'" (Matthew 15:22-23, CSB).

Comfort zones are a natural construct. We develop psychological, behavioral, and emotional boundaries that help define our daily lives. It's how we set our routines and are usually established for familiarity, safety, and security.

According to an article in Psychology Today, it is all part of a healthy adaptation for much of our lives.[28] The same article explains that it's also healthy (and necessary) to step beyond these comforts when "it's time to transition, grow, and transform."[29]

I love how much God connects various aspects of His creations. For example, we know that plants ultimately flower as a way of reproducing. It may seem weird, but they don't have to flower, and there are times that, when the conditions are perfect with no stress, they don't. They'll continue to be green and happy, but they don't produce a single bud. It's not until they feel stress–changes in temperature or changes in water–that those buds appear as survival instincts kick in for the plant. By flowering, they are able to mix pollen with other varieties and ultimately create a mix in plants that later grow that will be better to withstand the changes in the environment.

We're like plants in this. When everything is easy and comfortable, we'll continue to live but we won't ever be able to develop into our fullest potential. The slightest change might send us into a tailspin and destroy us. But by experiencing stressors and stepping outside of our comfort zones, we're able to transition and grow–better equipped to withstand the ever-changing environment around us.
To fully appreciate just how much this mother was reaching beyond her comfort zone, we need to look back at the history of the people of Israel and the Canaanites. The Canaanites—the descendants of Ham—were the people who occupied the land of Israel before the Israelites returned from Egypt. To understand the downfall of

---

[28] Brenner M.D., Abigail. "5 Benefits of Stepping Outside Your Comfort Zone." 12/27/2015 https://www.psychologytoday.com/us/blog/in-flux/201512/5-benefits-stepping-outside-your-comfort-zone. Accessed 11/8/2020.

[29] Ibid.

Canaan, we have to go back even further to the time just after the flood found in Genesis 9. Ham was the youngest son of Noah and dishonored him when he found him passed out drunk and naked. Noah responds to the insult by saying, "Cursed be Canaan; a servant of servants shall he be to his brothers" (Genesis 9:25, CSB). That may seem overly harsh, but it was a foretelling of the heart of the people who would later be called the Canaanites. They were a corrupt people that were involved in the worship of demonic idols, taboo sexual acts, and even child sacrifice to their false gods. Deuteronomy 9:5 explains that the Israelites weren't to overtake the Canaanites because they (the Israelites) were so wonderful and powerful, but because of the extreme wickedness of the other nation.

The Message version says it this way:

But when God pushes them out ahead of you, don't start thinking to yourselves, "It's because of all the good I've done that God has brought me in here to dispossess these nations." Actually it's because of all the evil these nations have done. No, it's nothing good that you've done, no record for decency that you've built up, that got you here; it's because of the vile wickedness of these nations that GOD, your God, is dispossessing them before you so that he can keep his promised word to your ancestors, to Abraham, Isaac, and Jacob (Deuteronomy 9:4-5, The Message).

So, a woman who can trace her lineage to a group of people so vile and wicked that God commanded the Israelites to dismantle their entire culture is approaching Jesus and begging for His help. But her lineage isn't merely Canaanite. She was specifically a Syrophoenician. Her race was a native of Phoenicia, the Roman province of Syria. She was from a mixed race that was heavily influenced by Greek culture. This Hellenistic influence was one of the key components that led to the shame culture that permeated the society in Jesus' life. It stole the voice of many, including women.

Are the lines that constrained her becoming a little clearer? Bottom line is that according to society, this woman had no right to speak to a man in this manner. According to history, this mixed-race, culturally detested individual had no right asking anything of a Jewish man. But Jesus transcends race and culture. He was not a blond-haired, blue-eyed, Caucasian that was so often portrayed across European cultures. He had left Jewish territory and was suddenly accessible to her and much like the woman who suffered from the issue of blood found in Mark 5, she reached out beyond her comfort zone, knowing that to experience the change she longed for, comfort zones needed to be crushed.

We're not so different from this woman. We know those things that make us comfortable—that help us feel safe. We so often settle because we are unwilling to step out and take the risk that comes from crushing comfort zones. I've had the pleasure and privilege to travel to several different countries and quite a few states throughout the U.S. My heritage is Southern, having grown up in a farming family in Florida. We in America like to call ourselves a melting pot of nationalities, but the reality is the "American" culture generally dominates over any true melding of other nations. We as a country are larger-than-life, proud to do it our way, and thought to be overly arrogant by many cultures throughout the world.

One of the countries I visited was Chad. This north central African nation is a mixture of Muslim culture combined with a number of native people groups who may or may not get along with one another. Before going on this trip, I was intimidated by the vast differences between their culture and my own. I knew that as a woman, I needed to present myself as more submissive. As an American, I needed to be overly respectful to counter the perception of the typical American tourist. I wasn't going to change who I was, but I wanted to be aware of the major differences and honor the fact that I was the guest. Being a foreigner, I was not required to dress a certain way but rather than balk at it, we chose to respect the traditions that were in no way challenging. I wore a scarf to cover my hair and long skirts whenever we were in public. When we deplaned at the airport in N'djamena, I kept my eyes down, not because I feared the heavily armed military men who were prominent from the tarmac through customs and even at the baggage claim, but out of respect for the cultural differences. My culture emphasizes eye contact as a form of respect and confidence, whereas it would have been taken as challenging authority in this culture.

But you don't have to travel halfway around the world to experience the act of crushing comfort zones. Sometimes it's as seemingly menial as adjusting to a different working style as you start a new job. Or perhaps it's when you are going to a new church that worships differently than how you grew up. When my husband and I got married, we both had to check our comfort zones at the door to establish what traditions and habits would work for our family unit apart from either of our parents or family histories.

Battle is not safe. It is not easy. It is not fun. This woman stood to be ridiculed and ignored and yet she still cried out. She didn't just ignore the comfort zones in her life; she shattered them. She continued her pleas until they took notice. There's something to be said about tenacity, but it's also important to acknowledge that she came before Jesus not with haughtiness and pride, but rather in humility.

APPROACH WITH HUMILITY AND KNOWLEDGE.

Because this woman was of a different race and culture, it wasn't expected that she would know the details of Jewish history and yet when she cries out to Jesus, she honors Him by calling Him, "Son of David." This title pulls from the Jewish prophecies of the coming Messiah. Isaiah 11:1 says, "Then a shoot will grow from the stump of Jesse, and a branch from his roots will bear fruit." Jeremiah also prophesied about the coming Messiah saying, "Look, the days are coming—this is the LORD's declaration—"when I will raise up a Righteous Branch for David. He will reign wisely as king and administer justice and righteousness in the land" (Jeremiah 23:4-5, CSB).

With a single title, this woman accomplished something even Jesus' own disciples had yet to do—identify Him as the prophesied Messiah and Savior of the Jews. Jewish men would have grown up memorizing these prophecies, but this woman wouldn't have been allowed to read them even if she had the capability to do so. Yet, she had a degree of knowledge that expanded beyond what was expected.

Again, her culture would not have taught her the Jewish scriptures and yet she seems to be walking in them. The book of Proverbs has plenty to say about humility. In chapter 11 verse 2 it says, "When arrogance comes, disgrace follows, but with humility comes wisdom" (CSB). Chapter 18 says, "Before his downfall a person's heart is proud, but humility comes before honor" (18:12, CSB). The psalmists also had plenty to say about approaching in humility. Psalms 25:9 says, "He leads the humble in what is right and teaches them His way" (CSB). Chapter 149 verse 4 says, "For the LORD takes pleasure in his people; He adorns the humble with salvation."

Of course, that psalm also addresses Jesus' somewhat perplexing response. Mark 7:27 tells us, "He said to her, "Let the children be fed first, because it isn't right to take the children's bread and throw it to the dogs." To the Jewish culture, dogs were often considered unclean, and they were unable to appreciate the value of a pet. While we might initially read this response as a tremendous insult there are multiple factors in place that actually allow these words to be encouraging.

First, let's address the children versus dog distinction. This wasn't meant to put her down, but rather establish the current differences in priority. Jesus was not shy about the fact that He came as the Jewish Messiah. He came to reach the people of Israel and to reaffirm them as the main root system that God established through His covenant with Abraham. Genesis 12 records God telling Abraham, "I will make you into a great nation, I will bless you, I will make your name great, and you will be a blessing. I will bless those who bless you, I will curse anyone who treats you with contempt, and *all people on earth will be blessed through you*" (Genesis 12:2-3, CSB, *emphasis mine*). The initial blessing would be on Abraham and his descendants but through his descendants—one in particular—all the earth would be blessed. Jesus echoes this when He says, "Let the children be fed first."

This isn't a matter of insult or telling her that she isn't worthy. This is a matter of His priority. Paul—who predominantly evangelized to the Gentiles (non-Jews)—continued this heart when he wrote, "For I am not ashamed of the gospel, because it is the power of God for salvation to everyone who believes, first to the Jew, and also to the Greek" (Romans 1:16, CSB). Jesus came to His original people, not to be exclusionary, but to set the precedence for all the others who would follow. The plan of the Gospel has always been to be for any and all, but God established the Israelites as His original people to establish a root system in which others could be grafted.

I've discovered that offense is all too easy to take on. Many people talk without thinking and in doing so will say something that can be taken differently than it was intended. While working my first job out of college, I focused on being thorough and competent, working toward a promotion within my first year. The company I worked for encouraged this and even competition within the different branches to push us to meet new sales goals. Shortly after I began working, a young man joined us at our branch. He was incredibly skilled in making sales, but I felt that he cut corners in integrity and customer service. While I never confronted him directly, I did feel offended every time the company rewarded him for his numbers, despite the fallout that I had to deal with in the form of customer complaints. Over the months we worked together, it gradually became more apparent that neither of us particularly liked working with the other.

While out running an errand with another coworker, I took the opportunity to ask him why exactly the other man did not like me or work well with me. He sheepishly responded that I could be "abrasive."

I knew I had asked the question and wanted an honest answer, but this one word caused a hurt in my heart for much longer than it should have. When thinking of the word "abrasive" all I could picture was a steel wool pad. You know what I'm talking about? They are the pads that if used incorrectly they can literally strip pots and pans, permanently damaging them. But here's the point—do you think this poor intern really meant to hurt me by implying that I permanently damaged people through my interactions with them? No. He was merely trying to explain that I was a strong personality and the young man in question was not used to working for a female superior. I hope that in the years since he has grown in maturity (as I hope the same for myself) and that he is able to appreciate what a woman in a position of authority can offer rather than balk against it.

As believers and warriors, we need to develop tough skin. There will be verbal attacks against us that hurt and are intended to do considerable damage—like how I let that evaluation of my character affect me for too many years. There will also be times when the words being said are not meant to cause offense, but if our hearts are not in line with God's will and design, we could take them the wrong way. Jesus wasn't looking to offend or insult this mother. He was merely using imagery—as was typical in the Middle Eastern manner of teaching—to explain His point.

In true humility the woman doesn't balk at Jesus' response or argue her worth. Instead, she does something that, again, goes against the expected response of an aristocratic Greek Canaanite, and bows at Jesus' feet. One commentary says that Matthew "uses this action as one befitting a king."[30] This act ties back to her earlier declaration of Jesus as the Son of David. In a single act she recognizes both His kingship and His authoritative power. Many before her had bowed before Jesus, asking for His healing or miraculous touch. It is a sign of submission and a form of worship.

We too need to kneel before our God and King. Worship is an integral form of battling the enemy's schemes. When we bow in worship to Jesus, we are submitting our hearts and wills before Him. We are actively acknowledging that He is the source of all power and authority. We are submitting to Him that we are His willing hands and feet, but the authority that we have been given is solely from Him. He is our source, and we can do nothing outside of Him. It is an act of faith.

HAVE FAITH TO BELIEVE.

The author of Hebrews tells us that faith is "the reality of what is hoped for, the proof of what is not seen" (11:1, CSB). The Gentile woman stepped beyond her comfort zone, came to Jesus with

---

[30] Works, Carla. Commentary on Matthew 15: [10-20]21-28. https://www.workingpreacher.org/preaching.aspx?commentary_id=2145. Accessed 10/21/2020.

knowledge but with full humility, and showed her level of faith in what Jesus could do and what she believed He would do for her. She hoped for a miracle to free her daughter from a demon and in acting on this faith she stepped into that place of proof of what is not seen.

Imagine you are this woman. Imagine your daughter is actively being tormented by a demon, day and night. Any mother knows that watching your child go through pain and suffering is, in many ways, more difficult than going through it yourself. You don't know what to do. You have sought help from local doctors and priests, but still she suffers. Then, in the whispering of gossip around the water well you hear someone mention a man who has cast out demons and healed the sick. You hear story after story about this Jewish Rabbi, who some speculate is the Jewish Messiah they have longed for and prophesied about for so many years. In those moments you wonder, could He possibly be this foretold king? Could He be the answer you are so desperate for?

In faith, she called out to Jesus—giving Him the most honoring title she knew. In faith, she continued her plea even in light of His disciples urging Him to dismiss her, claiming annoyance to her cries. In faith, she bowed before Jesus even after He told her no. In faith she persisted.

She didn't deny Jesus' statement. She didn't try to argue that she was a child as well—she knew she wasn't. She understood that He was there for the Jewish nation, but what is so amazing is that she sees beyond that specific priority and manages to understand God's heart for all His creation.

He replied, 'I was sent only to the lost sheep of Israel."

But she came, knelt before Him, and said, "Lord, help me!"

He answered, "It isn't right to take the children's bread and throw it to the dogs."

"Yes, Lord," she said, "yet even the dogs eat crumbs that fall from their master's table" (Matthew 15:24-27, CSB).

A woman from the wrong culture and race saw what so many of the chosen people of Israel did not. She saw that God had sent His Son to be the prophesied Son of David—King of the Jews—and while He came to redeem His chosen people, His power far surpassed that. She understood that even a crumb, cast off to the side—unwanted by its intended—was more than enough to fulfill the need she had.

Just prior to this interaction, Matthew 15 tells us about another conversation Jesus had with the Pharisees and scribes. In this exchange, the religious leaders were caught up on the details and missed the heart (a common occurrence for them). Jesus calls them out for their hypocrisy—worrying more about whether the disciples had washed their hands rather than if they were honoring their elders—and then tells the crowd, "Listen and understand: It's not what goes into the mouth that defiles a person, but what comes out of the mouth—this defiles a person…But what comes out of the mouth comes from the heart, and this defiles a person. For from the heart come evil thoughts, murders, adulteries, sexual immoralities, thefts, false testimonies, slander. These are the things that defile a person; but eating with unwashed hands does not defile a person" (Matthew 15:11, 18-20, CSB). From this exchange Jesus accomplishes two things: He emphasizes that He was more concerned with what is in the heart than doing everything exactly right and that cleanliness was going to expand beyond the confines of what the religious leaders understood.

The traditional Hebrew understanding of the heart derives from the word "lev." It implies more than simply the muscle inside our chest.

Instead, it relates to the seat of our thoughts, emotions, and intuitions. The combination of the two letters that comprise the word literally read as the voice of authority inside the tent, or the body of man. It's the place where you make your choices. This is why Jesus emphasizes that evil comes not from what we put in our mouths but from what overflows from our hearts. Goodness or evil will be evident in the choices we make, according to the thoughts, emotions, and intuitions we've allowed to take root inside us.

The Gentile mother may have been ceremonially unclean because of her culture but her heart was pure. She was acting in true faith and Jesus is always more concerned with the status of the heart than the ethnic boundaries and worldly restrictions we have erected.

We can't go into battle against the schemes of the devil without faith. It's even cataloged in the list of armor Paul writes about in his letter to the church in Ephesus. "In every situation take up the shield of faith with which you can extinguish all the flaming arrows of the evil one" (Ephesians 6:16, CSB). Faith is an action—something to be taken up and readily used against attacks. Imagine how arrows are used in battle. Often, they are volleyed toward the opposition from a distance, seeking to weed out as many adversaries as possible before getting closer where hand-to-hand combat would occur. It's a first line of offense, most effective at the onset of the battle.

Consider those offenses you might be clinging to, even years after the fact. Or those annoyances that cause you to respond with less kindness and patience. Or maybe those serious grievances that you've tried to surrender to God, but they just keep creeping up in your memory and everyday life. Those are flaming arrows. Paul is telling us that the shield of faith is capable of extinguishing each and every one shot against us if we are willing to pick it up and put it to use.

Jesus responds to the Gentile mother, "Because of this reply, you may go. The demon has left your daughter" (Mark 7:29, CSB). Matthew says it this way, "'Woman, your faith is great. Let it be done as you want.' From that moment her daughter was healed" (Matthew 15:28, CSB).

Because of her faith. Because she insisted in humility. Because she was willing to step beyond her comfort zone in the first place. Because of these key components, her daughter found relief and healing from the demon that was tormenting her. How can we follow her example? How can we push beyond comfort zones to give room for growth? How can we walk in both knowledge and humility, approaching others graciously but tenaciously? How can we pick up our shield of faith and extinguish the arrows the enemy is not only firing at us but at those closest to us? Our shields can protect more than just ourselves. Those closest to us benefit from our faith as well.

This battle is being fought on multiple fronts, in an exponential number of formats, but we are not left to wander aimlessly without the proper training or tools. God has equipped us in who we are, given us implements to wage war, and taught us the techniques that will bring us into the victory He has already secured. Even those women whose names are unknown have a story to tell. Even if no one knows your name, you too have a vital role to play. Are you willing to step up and lead?

"GOD HAS EQUIPPED US IN WHO WE ARE, GIVEN US IMPLEMENTS TO WAGE WAR, AND TAUGHT US THE TECHNIQUES THAT WILL BRING US INTO THE VICTORY HE HAS ALREADY SECURED."

CHAPTER SIX
FORTITUDE OVER FUNCTION
HAGAR | GENESIS 16

Hagar doesn't fit into the premise that I created for this book of the unknown or at least lesser-known women in scripture. In fact, many who grew up in the church are quite familiar with her—or they think they are. Unfortunately, we really only know her by her titles. We know her as Ishmael's mother. We know her as Abraham's second wife. We know her as Sarah's servant. We think of her as the woman who got in the way of God's promise. But do we really know her? Do we really know why she was included in the telling of the story?

The relationship between Abraham and Sarah's servant, Hagar, is one that many believers prefer to overlook. First, she is forced to sleep with Abraham and become a second wife whose sole purpose is bearing a son for the infertile primary wife. Ancient laws dictated that any child born to a servant would belong to Sarah and Abraham. This is why Sarah willingly gave her to Abraham. She was focused on man's understanding of God's promise rather than believing the impossible through God. Secondly, Hagar runs away because of how poorly she is treated by Sarah after conceiving and bearing that desired son. We don't know the extent of what she suffered. We don't know if she went willingly with Abraham or not. We don't know exactly what Sarah did or said that finally pushed her to the point of running away. What we do know is that there is no way to justify abuse. There is no way to explain away through culture or the time period that what she suffered was "okay" in any way. It wasn't. We don't know why she had to go through these challenges, but due to knowing the character of God as just and merciful, He would not have sent her back to an abusive situation. While there was likely still strong tension between Hagar and Sarah (proven by Sarah telling Abraham to cast them out later in the story), we can trust that there was some form of heart change in everyone involved to prevent further abuse. God never condones the abuse of another.

What we do know is that God uses imperfect people to advance His Kingdom. The Bible is full of imperfect people. There is example after example of individuals whom we've raised to elevated statuses where God never did. Abraham is honored by God not because he never made mistakes, but because he had faith to believe God. The uncomfortable conversation of Hagar and her role is one that we need to have without creating excuses. We aren't saying what Abraham did was right (in fact God makes it crystal clear that it wasn't), and we aren't excusing Sarah for her role either. Just as none of us are without sin, neither are any of the individuals in the Bible, besides Jesus. He is the only one who ever was and ever will be sinless. However, just as we can learn and grow from our own mistakes, we can learn and grow from the mistakes of others—including those whose names are incorporated in Hebrews 11's "hall of faith."

In this case, we're looking at Hagar's life—not Abraham's nor Sarah's, though both have plenty from which we could learn. Hagar's history is mostly unknown, though some scholars believe that she was of Egyptian origin, joining Abraham and Sarah after seeing how God intervened on their behalf (another prime example that these two spiritual "greats" made a lot of mistakes). According to Midrash (a Jewish commentary of the Torah), Hagar was not only Egyptian, but the daughter of the pharaoh[31]. If this was true, she willingly gave up her pampered freedoms to serve a foreign people whose foreign God proved himself to be real and alive—something none of the hundreds of her gods had ever managed.

Perhaps becoming the second wife was her end goal, as it would have still been a place of great honor and protection. Perhaps she was excited for the opportunity to step into a better role than simply that of a servant. In that time, a woman's main and most important purpose was to have children. This was the opportunity to fulfill that role and elevate her status in a single act. But in the end, it led to further ostracization. In the end, it propelled her to run off into the wilderness.

The wilderness is often seen as a negative. It's barren. It's lonely. It's difficult. But scripture shows us that many times the wilderness is the very place where we encounter God in new ways; where we can see and hear Him more clearly. This was true for Hagar as well. As a woman, she too was an ezer-warrior and through her story we can learn more about who we are as ezers.

WE ARE SEEN.

We are introduced to Hagar the day she is given to Abraham as a second wife. Genesis 16 tells us, "He slept with Hagar, and she became pregnant. When she saw that she was pregnant, her mistress became contemptible to her" (Genesis 16:4, CSB). Contempt is an

---

[31] Chabad.org/library/article_cdo/aid/112053/jewish/Hagar.htm. Accessed 8/17/2020.

interesting word in this case. The definition means to feel that a person is beneath consideration—that they are worthless.

Hagar was on the receiving end of what she had desired: fulfilling her societal role to become a wife and mother. She was no longer simply a slave in their household, but a woman of significance as the future mother of Abraham's first-born child. If she were in fact the daughter of the pharaoh, it's easy to see how she would see this as her opportunity to step back into a role she believed was her right, looking down on all other women in the household—including Sarah. But pride is a tricky thing. Proverbs warns us that "Pride comes before destruction, and an arrogant spirit before a fall" (Proverbs 16:18, CSB). Her spiteful attitude toward Sarah was unfortunately returned to her in spades. Sarah complains to Abraham who merely tells her to do what she wants with Hagar. Verse six says,

Abram replied, "Look, she is your servant, so deal with her as you see fit." Then Sarai treated Hagar so harshly that she finally ran away.
T
he angel of the LORD found Hagar beside a spring of water in the wilderness, along the road to Shur. The angel said to her, "Hagar, Sarai's servant, where have you come from and where are you going?" (Genesis 16:6-8, NLT).

Pregnant, alone, and likely afraid, Hagar encountered God.

Sometimes, we can feel alone, even when surrounded by people physically. I previously mentioned the serious car accident I was in with my three children in 2016. During that season, I remember having days where I felt completely disconnected from everyone around me. My oldest daughter, who sustained a broken neck and extensive ligament damage, may have made it through the most uncertain stages of her injury, but there were so many unknowns in her future. We didn't know how long she would have to wear the halo vest as the bones in her neck healed. We didn't know if there would be additional surgeries needed. We didn't know what she would be cleared to do when all was said and done. Despite having my husband's unyielding support, I would find myself detached— emotionally alone and wasting away. I had never been more scared than I was in those first hours following the car crash when I feared my oldest daughter might die, but the residual fear clung to me despite the strong face I put on for anyone who asked after me. It felt as if everything inside of me had been shredded and those aggravated wounds were prodded every time the insurance company called with more questions, or when we had to drive down to the hospital for another issue (or even just a follow-up visit). I intentionally avoided the street where the accident had occurred, but still dealt with anxiety attacks crippling my mind when cars would seem to be too close to me or appear to not see me while driving. I had to pull over, pleading and praying for my lungs to open as I struggled to catch my breath, eyesight blinded by a waterfall of tears, head pounding like it was caught in a vise. It wasn't the same fear I felt immediately following the crash, but it was debilitating and isolating—knowing that no one around me knew quite the extent to which I was suffering, nor how to help me.

But like Hagar, in that place of mental isolation, God met with me.

Psalms 56:8 says, "You've kept track of all my wandering and my weeping. You've stored my many tears in your bottle—not one will be lost. For they are all recorded in your book of remembrance" (TPT). Traditionally, Jewish women had what was called a lachrymatory, or a tear jar. This small jar was to physically collect their tears as a symbolic representation of collecting their emotions to then pour out in worship, faith, and trust. Emotions are a gift from God—not something to be shoved down and ignored. Yes, we need to maintain self-control (as a gift of the Spirit), but our emotions aren't wrong. This Psalm tells us that God keeps track of those tears; that He knows and empathizes with us in our pain.

Going back to Hagar's story, Genesis 16:7 says that the angel of the LORD (understood to be Jesus) found Hagar near a spring in the desert. In that fear and isolation, she ran into the wilderness. Too often we associate the wilderness with separation from God—the desert equaling God's desertion of us. But that is so far from the truth. The wilderness is not a place of desertion but rather a place to encounter God in new ways.

Look at Hosea chapter two. This beautiful story tells us how God continually pursues His people. In it we see Him saying, "Therefore, I am going to persuade her, lead her to the wilderness, and speak tenderly to her. There I will give her vineyards back to her and make the Valley of Achor into a gateway of hope. There she will respond as she did in her youth, as in the day she came out of the land of Egypt" (Hosea 2:14-15, CSB).

Hagar needed to be in the wilderness, away from the responsibilities that burdened her, away from the opinions of others that were crushing her, and away from the constant reminder of who she was not. She needed to be in the wilderness to instead receive the promises from a God who saw beyond the surface. God drew her into His presence to speak tenderly and to then challenge her to return. You see, just like it said in Hosea that God would give back her vineyards, for Hagar to receive that, she would have to return. We read in verses 9-10 of Genesis 16 that God told Hagar to return to Sarah. Being seen doesn't equate to life being easy. It means that no matter the circumstances, we know that God is with us and that God is for us. It means that no matter the circumstances, we can believe the character of God—often represented in His names.

WE ARE CALLED TO NAME.

In a culture where names are typically chosen simply because we like the sound of it, it's easy to forget that in Jewish culture (and many others), names are chosen based on their meaning. It is a way to speak over the life of that child and, in a way, prophesy over who they will become.

My family chose my sister and my names to give honor to other women in our family. My middle name, Anne, was chosen for my great aunt who was a bright light in my mom's memories as a child. She is a strong woman who isn't afraid to speak her mind. My sister's middle name, Ruth, is for our great-grandmother who was one of the most gracious women I've ever known while still having incredible quiet strength that she carried all 102 years of her life— an opinion shared by most who knew her. Ironically, both my sister and my personalities lend themselves to our namesakes.

When my husband and I chose names for our children, we decided to look at the meanings of the names. Our oldest, Samara, has already lived through a testimony of her name which means, "God protects," when she survived the injuries from the car accident despite the incredibly high mortality rate of those injuries. Aliyah, which means "exalted," was chosen as a prayer that her life would exalt God to those around her. Eli, which simply means "my God," equally goes by his middle name, Javier. Javier can mean "bright" or "new house." Again, we pray that his life will reflect God brightly and that he will walk boldly through life filled with the Holy Spirit.

In Genesis 16:13, we find Hagar responding to God's promise for her son, "So she named the LORD who spoke to her: 'You are El-Roi,' for she said, 'In this place, have I actually seen the one who sees me?'" Names have meaning. The names of God speak to His character and His power. Here, in the wilderness, a slave and a foreigner encounters God and experiences the wonder of being seen by the Most High.

It's not just our children that we name. We have the power and authority to name truth in our lives. We have the ability to call out the names of who God is in our lives and see His character firsthand as we encounter Him like Hagar did. I don't believe it was a coincidence that the first task given to Adam was to name the creatures God created.

God is the creator. He delights in making things new and likewise, He delights in drawing us into partnering with Him in His creation. Genesis 2 says, "The LORD God formed out of the ground every wild animal and every bird of the sky, and brought each to the man to see what he would call it. And whatever the man called a living creature, that was its name" (Genesis 2:19, CSB). God is the ultimate Father, wanting to play and engage with His children and this is proof. God fashions these astounding animals together and then lets Adam choose the name.

"Um...let's call it a Hippopotamus! And that one can be...Rhinoceros!"

I can imagine God laughing and responding, "Those are incredible names! You're so creative."

Smiling, feeling more confident, Adam continues and continues and continues. Creature after creature is brought before him and even as he clearly loses his creative juices, God remains the ever-encouraging Father.

"Here's an especially unique creature. One day people will say that based on its body size and wing size it shouldn't be able to fly, but it will. It'll help spread beauty through pollination, allowing flowers and plants to bloom and grow all over. What should we name it?"

"I don't know. How about bee?"

Me as a parent would look at him and again explain how amazing this creation was. How unique and special its role was despite its small stature. I'd press for something more substantial than "bee." But the Bible tells us that whatever the man called it, that was its name. God knew the power that came from naming things and wanted to establish that role for us from the very beginning.

Proverbs 18:21 says, "Death and life are in the power of the tongue, and those who love it will eat its fruit." We get the choice of whether we eat from life or eat from death. The words we say have great power and authority.

James says it this way:

We all fail in many areas, but especially with our words. Yet if we're able to bridle the words we say we are powerful enough to control ourselves in every way, and that means our character is mature and fully developed. Horses have bits and bridles in their mouths so that we can control and guide their large body. And the same with mighty ships, though they are massive and driven by fierce winds, yet they are steered by a tiny rudder at the direction of the person at the helm. And so the tongue is a small part of the body yet it carries great power! Just think of how a small flame can set a huge forest ablaze. (James 3:2-5, TPT)

The saying, "Sticks and stones may break my bones, but words can never hurt me," is nice in theory, going along with the idea of acting like a duck and letting words roll off you like water off a duck's back, but the reality is that words matter. A great deal. We were made in the image of God and our creator made all things *through His words*. John begins saying, "In the beginning was the Word...." (John 1:1a, CSB).

This power and authority are in even the smallest pieces of us—including our tongues. How can we take this truth and utilize it in our battles against the enemy? Sometimes it's as basic as speaking against the schemes of the enemy. When we are facing trials, we can speak against them, instead claiming the character and promises of God. In case that idea is foreign to you, let me give you an example. When our daughter was in the hospital with her broken neck and even after she came home in a halo vest, we would lay hands gingerly on her spine and then speak the words from Ezekiel 37 where God commanded the prophet to speak to the valley of dry bones and command them to come together—to come to life. We were praying for complete healing over her neck and even in the uncertainty of what was ahead, we used our words to prophesy in faith. This was new to me, having been raised in more traditional denominations, but as I grow in my faith, God continues to push me beyond my comfort zones into places where my faith must exist without borders. Does it line up with His word? Does it match His character? Then it can be acceptable and pleasing to God—even if it wasn't what I knew before.

Another example was when I felt led to anoint my house and pray for protection over it and all who were within. A couple weeks into the COVID-19 quarantine of 2020, I was feeling anxious and unsure. There were just so many unknowns and as someone who wants to see all my options, I felt blinded and unprepared. God gave me a vision of an angel wing—enormous in both size and strength—encompassing my entire home. He spoke to me words of protection over my family despite the fear being spread by the media. So, in faith, I got up, grabbed my bottle of Frankincense oil, and began to speak those same promises out loud as I spread the oil over the door frames of my home. The oil and the act were more symbolic than a requirement, but I felt God leading me to speak the prayer out, commanding any disease to leave in Jesus' name.

This isn't a magic spell. It isn't a checklist to ensure we get what we want. Speaking God's truth is an act of faith—a way to come into agreement with who God is and what He has said. If my daughter's bones hadn't been miraculously healed (which they were), it wouldn't be a sign of us not having enough faith or of saying the wrong words. It would simply be a different answer. The Bible says we see in part, so we prophesy in part (1 Corinthians 13:9). Sometimes, God is calling us to speak out His names so that we are reminded of His character despite our circumstances. Sometimes it's less about the words themselves, and more about the change that we allow those words to have in our own hearts and minds. Sometimes, we are called to name so that God can also remind us that we are more than our titles.

WE ARE MORE THAN A TITLE.

I began this chapter acknowledging that much of what we think we know about Hagar are simply her titles. Servant, Ishmael's mother, the other woman. In a culture where a woman's entire worth was heavily tied to her roles as wife and mother, it is often challenging to see beyond those.

Before she was Ishmael's mother, she was a servant to Sarah. Before she was in service to Sarah, she was an Egyptian woman who was looking for something more. She was convinced her value was in what she could provide—in her function and titles within Abraham's tent. But God saw her in the wilderness. He promised her that she would have a son and that, despite being stubborn and unruly, he would have a multitude of descendants. He heard her cry for purpose and proved it in the name of her son, Ishmael, which means God will hear. He gave her direction for this purpose—go back to your mistress and submit to her authority. Live under Abraham's protection and remain humble in this season.

The following years, Hagar remained. She raised her son as Abraham's first born and saw God continue to work through the destruction of Sodom and Gomorrah, His intervening after Abraham makes the same mistake of calling Sarah his sister in the presence of King Abimelech, and ultimately through the miraculous birth of Isaac. Unfortunately, around the time that Isaac is weaned, Ishmael is caught mocking his half-brother. Sarah, being a momma bear, fights to protect her young son. Abraham, being father to both, feels conflicted. God being over all things, gives assurance. He tells Abraham that the promise will be through Isaac but not to worry about Ishmael, for he, too, would be a great nation. So, Abraham sends Hagar and Ishmael away to the wilderness yet again.

There, with the water and her hope both gone, she cries loudly. And there in the wilderness, the angel of God calls out to Hagar. In her first encounter with God, Hagar named Him the God who sees. In her second encounter with God, He opened Hagar's eyes to see.

"'Get up, help the boy up, and grasp his hand, for I will make him a great nation.' Then God opened her eyes, and she saw a well" (Genesis 21:18-19, CSB).

He had promised her hope for her son the first time, but circumstances had clouded her vision. She was distraught that she had lost her position as second wife and now she was scared she would lose her son as well—the two titles that gave her the most value were being stolen from her.

Positions and titles can be valuable assets to our lives. They can be a sign of favor from God as He promotes us to new areas of influence whether in our jobs or in our homes. If I were to be asked who I was, the answer would often depend on where I was at the time. If I were picking my kids up from the kid's ministry at church, I would be Samara, Aliyah, or Eli's mom. If I were at a party for my husband's team from work, I'd be Kyle's wife. If I were visiting my extended family in Florida, I would likely be Kay and Charlie's younger daughter. If I were working a conference at our church, I'd be one of the adult ministry coordinators at the North Fort Worth campus. All these titles explain to the audience asking who I am and why I'm there. Those titles give me permission to be where I am.

Titles give clarification for our qualification, but they are rarely comprehensive. I am a mom, wife, and daughter. All of those are part of who I am but none of them is a complete picture of me. I am also a writer, speaker, administrator, teacher, friend…you get the idea. We're all made up of many titles, but only one can encompass who we truly are: daughter of God. It is less a question of who we are and more a truth in Whose we are.

Hagar was no longer a wife in Abraham's household, but she was still seen by God. As her son grew in strength, she was no less his mother, but that role changed, and God was always with them. Our value and worth are not in the titles we hold. They can change and will shift in each season of our lives, but the rock-solid truth that we are God's daughters—beloved, chosen warriors—will never change. That will carry us into eternity with our Heavenly Father, giving us confidence to fight our battles despite the changing circumstances.

He is telling us, like Hagar, to get up. Grasp the hands of the blessings and promises He has already spoken over your life and walk out your life knowing those as truths that won't be stolen from you. Lift your eyes from where they are overwhelmed by trials and tears. Allow Him to open your eyes to see the wellspring of life that is Jesus—our Living Water, the one who refreshes our soul, washes us clean, and makes us new in His image.

"WE'RE ALL MADE UP OF MANY TITLES, BUT ONLY ONE CAN ENCOMPASS WHO WE TRULY ARE: DAUGHTER OF GOD. IT IS LESS A QUESTION OF WHO WE ARE AND MORE A TRUTH IN WHOSE WE ARE."

CHAPTER SEVEN
THE UNEXPECTED WARRIOR
JAEL | JUDGES 4

I t's all too easy to feel unseen. It's all too easy to allow our circumstances to overwhelm us. It's all too easy to claim that someone else will fight–we don't really have to do it. What is easy can just as easily be a lie from the enemy. As we talked about with Hagar, we are seen and we are so much more than whatever is going on in our lives. Our titles and our circumstances do not define us. In fact, we are called to name those blessings in our life to bring them to the forefront.

When we look at a story, the main character can just as readily be an unknown as in an established position. Truthfully, I've read more books that begin with someone unknown or at least displaced from their rightful position, than one's where the main character is already in the necessary position to accomplish all that is expected of them by the end of the story. Our lives are more than a fairy tale, movie, or play, but I use this analogy because we are in the midst of the most epic story ever created. That's what this is all about– discovering who we've been created to be, what tools and characteristics we've been given to succeed, and what it is we've been called to do.

I have this somewhat-secret desire to be trained in all things battle related. I blame it on the fact that I enjoy fantasy fiction and all the best ones inevitably include epic sword fighting, spectacularly accurate shooting of bows and arrows, and this journey where the main character starts off weak and incapable only to become strong, fierce, and able to take on the battle before them. I think it's the strong part I most resonate with. It is this idea that I can work and train my mind and my muscles to overcome impossible obstacles, saving the kingdom and possibly even the world. Okay, I really don't aspire to save the world, but I would love to learn to shoot a bow and arrow and be able to attack a Tough Mudder course with confidence and the endurance to match.

I don't think I could write a book called Skull Crushers without this woman being included. Jael wasn't the main character in the story. Truth be told, she wasn't even supposed to be in the story. It begins with the current judge for Israel, Deborah, and one of her military commanders, Barak. They were the ones who went to war. They were the ones to confront the Canaanites who had been oppressing Israel for the past 20 years. It's not always the obvious main character who plays a vital role in the story.

We are all playing a role in this story. We all have a part and sometimes it's prominent and in the spotlight, while other times it feels like we're the forgotten extra hiding backstage. No one has been forgotten. God has prepared an interaction or relationship or conversation just for you. He has a plan and a purpose for you that goes beyond what we can fathom.

For Jael, it literally stumbled into her backyard, but she was ready to do what needed to be done, and for that all of history knows her name.

HE HAS CALLED US UP.

Jael was a common girl. She was not a warrior. She wasn't even on the battlefield. "Meanwhile, Sisera had fled on foot to the tent of Jael, the wife of Heber the Kenite, because there was peace between King Jabin of Hazor and the family of Heber the Kenite" (Judges 4:17, CSB). Jael was at home, going through her normal day and normal routine. She wasn't looking for glory, but when her circumstances shifted, she accepted them and took care of the issue that was brought literally to her doorstep.

If we look back a few verses, we see a little foreshadowing. "Now Heber the Kenite had moved away from the Kenites, the sons of Hobab, Moses' father-in-law, and pitched his tent beside the oak tree of Zaanannim, which was near Kedesh" (Judges 4:11, CSB). This family was descended from Moses' father-in-law, but for whatever reason they had moved from where they had traditionally resided. The Kenites weren't involved in the war between the Israelites and the Canaanites, so it makes sense why in a culture that prioritizes hospitality, Sisera would have presumed he would be sheltered and cared for in Jeal's tent. Maybe at another time, he would've been. But this circumstance was ordained by God to go a different way.

There are a lot of things in our world that while considered culturally acceptable do not bring God honor. If you're unsure, think about those things that the world praises and causes different churches to battle each other on what is or is not acceptable according to scripture. For all of these, the most important thing to remember is to not make the person equate to the sin. Sin is what we do, not who we are. Jesus desperately loves all of us, while still detesting the sins that keep us from being in perfect union with Him. The Bible says, "For *all* have sinned and fall short of the glory of God" (Romans 3:23, emphasis mine). We have no right to judge another person based on whether his or her sin is on our personal list of "major sins" or not because that's not our role. That's one of the reasons I'm not listing any specific examples. Instead, I want to challenge each of us to look at our own hearts and lives. Is there something that scripture tells us is against God but that we've allowed to be acceptable to us because it fits with our current culture?

In the fall of 2021, I helped facilitate a class called Sexual Integrity.[32] While this course specifically uses sexual addictions in their examples, the reality is that addictions can be to anything: sex, drugs, food, our phones, etc. It's less about the specific vice and more about removing the shame surrounding the struggle so that we can draw it out into the light and find healing. Neurologically, addictions follow a certain pattern no matter what it is the person is addicted to. It's less about the specific sin and more about the heart. Why are we falling victim to that temptation? Why are we looking for comfort in that way? Again, the person is not the sin. God loves the person and despises the sin because that is what is causing the separation from Him.

We as created beings, reflecting a Triune God, are in fact composed of three parts: body, soul, and spirit. Our body is what the Bible calls the flesh. Flesh and blood we get. We can understand that when our stomach grumbles, we're hungry. When our finger gets slammed in a door, it hurts. The soul is our mind, will, and emotions. Finally, our spirit is that eternal piece that is our direct line to our Creator.

When we don't have a relationship with God, all three parts are dictated by the body. The idea of "do what feels good" would fall in line with this. Then there are some people who don't know Jesus, but we would still call them "good people." They are generous and kind to others. They are considerate and self-sacrificing. These

---

[32] Puredesireministries.org

individuals would be ruled by their souls. Their mind and emotions dictate their decisions and that allows them to be more aware than people who are simply ruled by their fleshly desires. Finally, we have believers who are in a genuine relationship with God. They are ruled by their spirits. Their spirit is in communion with the Holy Spirit, and it allows them to respond from an eternal perspective.

What part of you is in control? You might be a believer but if you have never fully surrendered your will to God, you'll find that it's not your spirit leading you, but your soul. You might know the Father, but you have bondage that is preventing His Spirit from being able to fully guide you. I didn't realize it until years later, but this was my reality through my college years.

I accepted Jesus as my Savior when I was eight years old. I knew the love of God and walked in confidence of that truth. Unfortunately, I never fully surrendered my life to His will. For much of the time, I was still a good kid and made decent choices, but there were other times that I fell to the desires of my flesh and opened myself to the meddling of the enemy in my life. I was secretive and deceptive. I found myself in relationships that didn't honor God and were instead a part of what I later determined was an addiction to love. I wasn't addicted to sex, but I was addicted to the idea of love and thus willing to do whatever I needed to do to keep someone I thought loved me. It wasn't until I began to recognize the spiritual warfare going on against me and break the bondage that I began to see change. My life shifted from being led by my soul (which overpowered everything else), and my spirit took the reins. It allowed clearer communication with God and a better understanding, so it was no longer my opinion of good and right, but God's. I was called to be set apart—be brought higher. We all are.

Jael's name means *mountain goat* which seems very mediocre and not a remarkable thing to be named after, but it is derived from a root word that means *to ascend*. God has called us to be sanctified or set apart. We have a calling to not just be mediocre–like we might consider a goat to be–but to be more, to rise above. The best news is that this isn't something that we have to do by our own power but is done by God in us.

HE HAS EQUIPPED US.

My dad is really skilled at hanging things on the wall. That may sound a little sarcastic, but I mean it genuinely. My mom loves decorating the house and has an HGTV-level knack for it. This means pictures change out, decorations switch with the seasons, and there are sometimes unusual requests for atypical objects to be hung on the wall. I'd like to say that I inherited these skill sets–both the vision to decorate and the skill to accomplish my vision. I may have gotten a fraction of them. I get really good ideas, but my execution is, let's just say, questionable. Currently, I have this vision for the master bedroom. It was the second room I painted, and now I'm wanting to create a picture collage on the wall that encompasses each year that my husband and I have been together. I have several pictures that are framed, but because I only have a few pictures printed and ready to go, I didn't preplan how the pictures were going to be hung. I also didn't have the proper hooks to hang the frames. I did have some nails though, so I decided to just wing it. I grabbed the nails, my handy hammer, and picked a spot on the wall. I also made the brilliant decision to download a level app onto my phone. I should probably let you know that I started this project last year. Currently, there are three pictures that are framed and hung, several others that I got framed but decided not to hang and have them on different shelves, but then I have two pictures that I haven't found frames for yet. I was worried that they would get ruined or lost if I just left them on my dresser, so I took some washi tape and taped them to the wall where I think they might someday end up. They've been that way for months.

There are situations that we feel readily prepared for and then other times there are circumstances that arise that we're left holding a hammer, some random nails, and some washi tape, and expected to just make it work. Just figure it out. Wing it.

Jael went out to greet Sisera and said to him, "Come in, my lord. Come in with me. Don't be afraid." So he went into her tent, and she covered him with a blanket. He said to her, "Please give me a little water to drink for I am thirsty." She opened a container of milk, gave him a drink, and covered him again. Then he said to her, "Stand at the entrance to the tent. If a man comes and asks you, 'Is there a man here?' say, 'No.'" While he was sleeping from exhaustion, Heber's wife, Jael, took a tent peg, grabbed a hammer, and went silently to Sisera. She hammered the peg into his temple and drove it into the ground, and he died. (Judges 4:18-21, CSB).

I'm intrigued by the details of this story. Jael invites him in, as the rules of hospitality would've dictated. She feeds him into a stupor, then once he's sound asleep, she takes the tent peg and drives it through his skull. Can we address the strength of both wit and body here? It's easy to look at situations that aren't life and death–like my decorating skills–and think, "I can just wing it." But what about those situations that affect so much more than my drywall? What about the situations that directly affect my family or the volunteers working with me on a project?

Working with the adult ministries department at my church has allowed me to see behind the curtain on the organization and execution of a number of events. Even events we hold on a weekly basis require detailed planning to execute successfully. We have contingency plans in place as well as designated individuals who are tasked with addressing problems as they arise. Has it been successful? Yes. Has it gone off each week without any issues? Absolutely not. The morning after any event includes a standing meeting in place to debrief. We take time to discuss what went well, what did not, and what we can do to address any concerns or issues that happened.

Jesus talks about "counting the cost" in Luke 14. He had healed a man on the Sabbath, then told two parables addressing humility and explaining that honor comes with sacrifice–trying to teach them that we aren't to elevate our own status but allow God to be the one to choose to exalt us if it will bring Him glory. He then continues on with acknowledging that being a follower of Him comes at great cost and sacrifice.

For which of you, desiring to build a tower, does not first sit down and count the cost, whether he has enough to complete it? Otherwise, when he has laid a foundation and is not able to finish, all who see it begin to mock him, saying, 'This man began to build and was not able to finish.' Or what king, going out to encounter another king in war, will not sit down first and deliberate whether he is able with ten thousand to meet him who comes against him with twenty thousand? And if not, while the other is yet a great way off, he sends a delegation and asks for terms of peace. (Luke 14:28-32, ESV).

An architect readily plans out the details of the space before he begins planning the actual structure. He partners with the engineers and construction supervisors to ensure what the cost will actually be and what is feasible to create. Likewise, a king strategizes the battle before a single soldier is lined up for war. The war council meets multiple times to consider every possibility and to look at different perspectives of each of those possibilities. They want to limit the loss of lives and maximize the potential of victory.

When Sisera arrived at Jael's tent, it may seem like she was winging it. It may seem like she didn't have the right tools and preparation to accomplish what she needed to do. But look back at what was said in verse 11, "Now Heber the Kenite had moved away from the Kenites, the sons of Hobab, Moses' father-in-law, and pitched his tent beside the oak tree of Zaanannim, which was near Kedesh" (Judges 4:11, CSB).

She was married to a member of a Bedouin people group. Moving wasn't abnormal. She would've been skilled at tearing down and erecting her tent with the others. Women had many responsibilities that required them to be physically strong and capable. Then the fact that they just so happened to move their tents near where the battle would take place seems a little coincidental, don't you think?

God will use what we see as just part of our everyday responsibilities to prepare us for the battle ahead. He can use your background in education and training to prepare you for parenting a child with special needs. He can use your skills working in a high-pressure office to know how to stay levelheaded in an emergency situation that has other people in a panic. He can use your history of being the recipient of bullying to start an organization that fights back and brings awareness to mental health and strategies to the community.

What skills do you already have at your disposal? What pieces of your everyday life might be turned into the right tools for the battle before you? How have you been uniquely equipped to crush the skull of the enemy?

This became a reality to me following the car accident I mentioned in earlier chapters that my kids and I were in. Like I said before, my oldest daughter, Samara, suffered the most severe injuries with several fractures to her neck and extensive ligament damage. At the time, I felt completely overwhelmed. I don't have any medical background, nor have I ever had any aspirations to work in the medical field. I was a stay-at-home mom of three littles. I had worked in ministry in several capacities, but nothing that would obviously prepare me for walking though months of recovery with her.

God, however, knew what was ahead of me. Only six months prior, I began to discover my prayer language. For those who are unfamiliar with this, it's a personal language that allows our spirit to commune more closely with the Holy Spirit. It's what Paul is referring to when he says, "Now if we hope for what we do not see, we eagerly wait for it with patience. In the same way the Spirit also helps us in our weakness, because we do not know what to pray for as we should, *but the Spirit himself intercedes for us with inexpressible groanings.* And he who searches our hearts knows the mind of the Spirit, because he intercedes for the saints according to the will of God" (Romans 8:25-27, CSB, *emphasis mine*). It's a form of tongues but meant for personal growth rather than the edification of others around us. That's why Paul also said in 1 Corinthians 14:2, "The man who speaks in special sounds speaks to God. He is not speaking to men. No one understands. He is speaking secret things through the power of the Holy Spirit" (NLV).

Not having grown up with this knowledge, it was a little weird when it seemed so common to others around me. At this point, I knew I had received the baptism of the Holy Spirit–that I was walking in communion with God, fully surrendered to His will over my own. Despite that, I didn't know how to get this personal language that would allow my spirit to be strengthened. Turns out, you just have to ask, which seemed easy enough. Only, I felt like I was making things up as I went. It wasn't until I heard God say, "Becca, release control. Stop trying to understand or create the words. Allow my Spirit to simply flow through you like the breath of life that He is."

I began by taking a deep breath and then breathing out, releasing my tongue to form whatever sounds and words that would flow out.

Little by little, I felt less weird about it. I have control over when I pray in tongues. It's not about losing control of myself but rather relinquishing the need to dictate the flow of my spirit. This may not be the same for everyone. Some people burst out speaking in tongues immediately upon receiving the baptism of the Holy Spirit as an overflow of His presence. Some never feel inclined to pray in tongues at all. This isn't required as proof of anything. This isn't something that has to be part of your arsenal to receive salvation. It's a way to stretch our spirits and grow closer to the heart of God. It allows us to intercede for things even when we don't know the details, but God does.

Jumping ahead those six months to the time we were going through the repercussions of our accident, I found myself dealing with challenges I felt wholly unprepared for. When I couldn't identify my own feelings beyond the anxiety, let alone put actual words to my prayers, I could commune with God through my prayer language. I could lay hands on my daughter's broken neck, pray for healing and so much more through the special sounds and words that meant nothing to my human mind but were worshiping God in my spirit. Don't forget that we are three parts: body, soul, and spirit. We can pray and worship God with all three if the spirit is the part that is in control. I may have had to learn medical jargon and become overly familiar with the local children's hospital, but I was already equipped to intercede for the miracle of her healing.

HE HAS HONORED US.

One of my favorite Disney movies is *Mulan* (the original cartoon one). The decision that she made to go to war in her father's place wasn't made from a heart of rebellion, but rather respect and love. She knew because of her father's previous injuries, he would likely die if he fulfilled the requirement issued by the emperor. She wasn't seeking to dishonor her family by dressing as a man and deceiving everyone she met. And in turn, by doing what she could to look out for her family, and eventually her troop and commander, she was honored by the emperor himself for her dedication, wit, and sacrifice.

Honor can mean to adhere to what is right, but it can also be reflected through a tribute which is defined as "something resulting from something else and indicating its worth."[33] The stories we tell, the lasting memories, the actions we take can all be tribute to people in our life–an attempt at showing the world their worth.

Sometimes it feels like we interchange respect with honor. While respecting someone can be a sign of honor, they aren't inherently the same. Respect is more about acknowledging someone or their position and acting accordingly. It's not really the same as acting in such a way as to show their value to others. I can respect someone's position without feeling that they should be honored. I may be splitting hairs here, but ultimately, I believe that honor is more than simply respecting someone. It is a clear recognition of their value and worth. Another way to look at it is that honor prompts a response. I can respect someone as a person or a position without being prompted to do anything about it. When I honor someone, I want my words and actions to reflect that.

Since I began working at our church, I have been intentionally meeting more people. Many of the group leaders now recognize me from different interactions and from trainings I've led, as well as from the times I've served on the weekend rotation during services. While my husband also volunteers, he has mostly served in our children's ministry and so many of the adult leaders don't recognize him. Instead, he has lovingly adopted the name of "Becca's

---

[33] Merriam-Webster.com Dictionary, s.v. "tribute," accessed May 21, 2022, https://www.merriam-webster.com/dictionary/tribute.

husband" at many events. He laughs about it and bears the title with grace as he is proud of the work I am doing. But more than anything, I want to honor him.

Not many of our current friends knew us when we first began dating in 2005. I was only a year removed from being in an extremely unhealthy relationship and a mess spiritually. Kyle was in his last year of college and not looking to stick around the area upon graduation. Despite our best efforts to ignore the growing attraction (Kyle even told me he prayed God would take it away), we fell for each other. What I didn't realize at the time was just how much baggage I was bringing into this relationship. The baggage from past relationships and my addiction to the idea of love made me slightly neurotic and very clingy. I reacted to the slightest disagreements by taking on a victim mentality and measured my self-worth by my relationship status rather than by the truth of who God called me to be.

Somehow, despite all of that, Kyle stuck with me. Not only that, but he introduced me to ways of gaining spiritual freedom and breaking off soul ties. He guided me and loved me in ways I had never experienced from any other relationship. Does that mean he was perfect? Of course not, but it was in those first few years that we experienced such highs and lows that since then most disagreements have seemed mellow in comparison.

When we got married and began having kids, I grew to love him even more as he stepped up time and time again to care for our family. When we were in the car accident, I struggled with anxiety to such a degree that I couldn't even fathom dealing with the mountain of paperwork and insurance details that were required. Kyle managed all of it. We parent as a team. We are best friends and I love him more today than I ever have. His care and love for me as a result of simply who he is shows me his worth. His pride in me and my job elevates that even further as I often don't feel deserving of his devotion. But in everything I do, the conversations I have, the stories I share (or don't), the way I react around him–I want it all to honor him. I want others to see just how valuable this man is.

Following the battle and subsequent discovery of Sisera dead in the tent of Jael, Deborah sings a song to memorialize what has just happened. Judges 5 says, "Most blessed of women is Jael, the wife of Heber the Kenite; she is most blessed among tent-dwelling women" (Judges 5:24, CSB). Deborah and Barak have just fought in this massive war, but Deborah took time to bring attention to the actions of Jael. Not only did she tell what Jael did and the result of her actions, but she called her most blessed among tent-dwelling women. Her status should have made her inclined to provide protection for an ally seeking refuge in her home. Instead, she stood with the people of Israel and through her actions, ensured peace over the nation for the next 40 years.

God, too, honors His ezer-warriors. Jesus told His followers, "**If anyone serves me, he must follow me; and where I am, there will my servant be also. If anyone serves me, the Father will honor him**" (John 12:26, CSB). When we devote our lives to Him, He blesses and honors us. When we surrender our hearts, allowing Him to guide us, we see that He is gracious to us, even in our weaknesses. We don't do it because we're going to be honored. In fact, Jesus warns about these people when He quotes Isaiah, "This people honors me with their lips, but their hearts are far from me" (Matthew 15:8, CSB). The Pharisees were so worried about doing the right actions, they ignored the fact that it was a heart issue above all else. We don't obey God to get something. We obey God because we love Him.

He honors us because He wants to. He wants to express His love for us and for us to know and understand how great His love is for us. And in turn we get to honor Him more and others around us, continuing the cycle until the day we will all be in heaven, bowing before the King of kings.

CHAPTER EIGHT
WISDOM HAS MANY FACES
THE WOMAN AT THE WALL | 2 SAMUEL 20

I f you've been in church for even a short amount of time, you're likely familiar with the woman at the well. She was the Samaritan woman who met with Jesus and because of her encounter, became the first missionary–running to tell her entire town about what Jesus had said to her and brought them back with her to have an encounter of their own. While there are certainly incredible truths we can learn from her, that is not who I am referencing in the title of this chapter. It's not a typo, but truly the woman at the wall. Her name is never listed, though that detail itself can be vital information for us.

When I read stories in scripture, or any history, I oscillate between being able to imagine myself walking in their shoes or struggling to comprehend how they managed the feats before them. My imagination is pretty good, but there are times when I know that there is no feasible way to fathom the depths of what someone journeyed through. My oldest daughter has a love for the imaginary.

She is at the crossroads of life as a pre-teen. One side longs to run headlong into the world of being a teenager and adult and the other side is grasping at the quickly disappearing childhood fancies. She wants responsibilities and privileges that come with growing up but loves the innocence and fun of childhood. Within this conflicting reality of her own world exists a vibrant story that she has created with her sister and regularly acts out. At any given moment they will traverse parallel realities of real life to the life and adventures of their universe of the light and dark, good versus evil, crazy royal families, and never-ending thrills between friends. What began as "stuffed animal stories" has morphed into a fantasy world with an excruciatingly detailed backstory. With an imagination like hers, she can read any story and immediately empathize with the characters.

Where my daughter excels in immersing herself into the character's life and challenges, I believe that one of the reasons we have so many unnamed characters in scripture is not because they were forgettable or unimportant, but because they were transversive. They were meant to relate to a broader audience than some of the people who have more of a backstory included. By leaving them nameless, we are better able to put ourselves in their shoes–even without an imagination like my daughter's.

There are two instances of a wise woman interceding and affecting the trajectory of events during King David's rule and both involve David's army commander, Joab. The first was sent by Joab to David to convince him to allow Absalom to return home. The second was on the heels of Joab subsequently killing Absalom, and amid chasing down another usurper trying to divide the kingdom. The women's roles vary, their approaches vary, but both were paired with the title of "wise." For this chapter, we're going to examine how the second woman, the woman at the wall, demonstrated how we as ezers need wisdom to battle the enemy before us and three ways to demonstrate that wisdom.

Proverbs tells us that wisdom is to be desired more than riches. "For wisdom is better than jewels, and all that you may desire cannot compare with her" (Proverbs 8:11, ESV). Proverbs 16 says it this way, "How much better to get wisdom than gold! To get understanding is to be chosen rather than silver" (Proverbs 16:16, ESV). But why?

Wisdom in and of itself is beyond simply having knowledge. There is one definition that states that it is having knowledge and knowing what to do with it. I wouldn't disagree, but again, that's not really a complete understanding. That definition still makes it plausible that wisdom is attainable by man's might alone–if we live enough life, have enough experiences, read enough books or articles or studies. But Godly wisdom is given by God alone–not by life. James 1:5 says, "If any of you lacks wisdom, you should ask God, who gives generously to all without finding fault, and it will be given to you" (CSB). That readily implies that wisdom is something that is given, not earned or acquired. Even Solomon, considered the wisest man to live, had to ask for wisdom:

"Your servant is among your people you have chosen, a people too many to be numbered or counted. So give your servant a receptive heart to judge your people and to discern between good and evil. For who is able to judge this great people of yours?"

Now it pleased the Lord that Solomon had requested this. So God said to him, "Because you have requested this and did not ask for long life or riches for yourself, or the death of your enemies, but you asked discernment for yourself to administer justice, I will therefore do what you have asked. I will give you a wise and understanding heart, so that there has never been anyone like you before and never will be again. In addition, I will give you what you did not ask for: both riches and honor, so that no king will be your equal during your entire life" (1 Kings 3:8-13, CSB).

God desires to give us wisdom and expand the territory that we can care for due to that wisdom. When we walk in His ways, trusting Him to guide us rather than leaning on our own understandings (Proverbs 4:6-7), utilizing discernment to recognize the difference between worldly knowledge and the truth that God leads us in, we're able to function from a place of wisdom. We're able to battle in that same place of wisdom, starting with recognizing who is in authority and honoring that position.

RECOGNIZE AUTHORITY.

This might not seem like it would fit in a book focused on empowering women in their roles as warriors, but the best soldier will tell you that it's vital to recognize authority and be submitted to it. This isn't true only for women, but everyone. We are all called to be submitted to the authority of Christ. Jesus tells one of the disciples in John 14, "Don't you believe that I am in the Father and the Father is in me? The words I speak to you I do not speak on my own" (John 14:10, CSB). Another version says, "The words I speak to you I do not speak on my own authority. Rather, it is the Father, living in me, who is doing his work" (NIV). Jesus himself was submitted to the authority of the Father. We as believers are then submitted to the authority of Christ. In Matthew 28:18, Jesus tells the disciples, "All authority has been given to me in heaven and on earth" (CSB). Then Colossians 2:9-10 says, "For the entire fullness of God's nature dwells bodily in Christ, and you have been filled by him, who is the head over every ruler and authority" (CSB).

The word Paul used for "head" in this verse from Colossians is interesting. In the Greek there are two different words used for head: *arche* and *kephale*. *Arche* may look familiar because of how often we see its prefix used–archangel, archenemy, archeology, etc. This word, simply translated as head, is more accurately used to reference the beginning or the first of something (particularly in importance). Knowing this, it would make sense if Paul used *arche* to describe Jesus being the head over every ruler and authority as he is certainly the most important and positionally above all. But that's not what he did. Instead, Paul used the other word: *kephale*. This does refer to the head of one's body and can also mean the most important in terms of position and hierarchy (see what I did with the word *arche* there?), but it is also used militaristically. Rather than meaning the general or most important person over the military, it references the soldier that went in first, in front of the troops. It refers to the one who was the first to enter the battle.

We as believers submit to Jesus not as a distant ruler, calling out directions and orders from a safe location, but as the one who willingly stepped into the battle first. He leads from a place of example and submission to the Father. Likewise, we have been called to submit to earthly authority in our lives as well. Titus 3:1 says, "Remind them to submit to rulers and authorities" (CSB). Romans 13:1-2 says, "Let everyone submit to the governing authorities, since there is no authority except from God, and the authorities that exist are instituted by God. So then, the one who resists the authority is opposing God's command, and those who oppose it will bring judgment on themselves" (CSB). This does not say that the rulers and authorities will always be Godly men and women who never do anything wrong, simply that there are times that God will allow people to come into power to ultimately bring about His glory and honor and it won't always make sense to us in the natural world. We don't see the full picture, but we are called instead to trust that God knows what He is doing and "...all things work together for the good of those who love God, who are called according to His purpose" (Romans 8:28, CSB).

Personally, I know this is hard. I have had to submit to people placed in positions of authority over me–whether as a group leader, project leader, boss, or other position—and I have greatly disagreed with them in both methodology and direction. Honestly, I haven't always handled this well. In one instance, I had a vice president of another department who was technically in a position of authority over me. I was a manager in a different department at the time and while I believed we had an understanding about my borrowing one of his employees for a training I needed help with, he went back on his word. A few days prior to the training I was informed that my co-worker would not be able to support me because her VP reprioritized her tasks. Feeling betrayed, I confronted the VP, but not in an honorable manner. I spoke in anger and hurt rather than reason and in doing so undermined any ground I might have achieved by instead acknowledging his position of authority and recognizing that whether I agreed to his decision or not, it was still his decision to make.

One of the best examples of honoring someone despite their not being honorable is in how David treated Saul. Throughout all of 1 and 2 Samuel, we see the progression of Saul being named king, then his demise and loss of the kingdom coinciding with David's rise and eventual acquisition of the kingdom of Israel. Saul was a prideful man who did what he wanted rather than submitting to the direction God gave. David in contrast, submitted to Saul as God's chosen king even after he was anointed as the next in line. Saul attempted to kill him multiple times, but even when there were ample opportunities to in turn kill Saul, David never laid a hand on him. He even went so far as to punish those who tried to do so.

The woman on the wall of Abel Beth Maacah began her reasoning by calling out to the man in the position of authority. Joab hadn't taken the position of leadership honorably, but he was the one the king's men were following. She didn't question his honor or his credentials. She didn't point out his corruption or demean him in any way. When she had his attention, she didn't demand he leave or stop the siege. Instead, she reasoned with what she knew and appealed to him as a man who understood both reason and the history of their city. She could have just called out to the masses attempting to win them over to her pleas, but instead she recognized that to accomplish anything, she needed to submit and recognize who was in a position of authority to pacify the attack.

Second Samuel 20 says, "...a wise woman called from the city, 'Listen! Listen! Tell Joab to come here so I can speak to him.' He went toward her, and she asked, 'Are you Joab?'

'I am,' he answered.

She said, 'Listen to what your servant has to say.'

'I'm listening,' he said" (2 Samuel 20:16-17, CSB).

Imagine how differently it would have gone if this woman instead just yelled at the troops to stop. Imagine her berating them about all the ways they were wrong, how their attack wouldn't yield the results they wanted, and how many innocents they would hurt in the process. Imagine her hurling insults at Joab instead of approaching him humbly. Instead of a request as a submitted person before him, if she came saying, "Your approach is all wrong and you're going to kill an entire city in the process! What's wrong with you?"

While she wouldn't have been wrong in what she was saying, I highly doubt Joab would have responded with something as level-headed as, "I'm listening."

The manner in which we approach people, especially those in positions of authority, matters. Every time David approached Saul, he bowed before him and called himself Saul's servant. When the woman on the wall called to speak with Joab, she did so with a request that he listen to his servant. Not a servant as someone less-than, but simply as someone who recognizes the authority given to them, that is, from a position of respect. We can honor people in a position of authority without degrading our own status. Reasoning with respect allows for a response of reason. When we offer respect, people are more receptive to reason with us and hear what we have to say.

CLARIFY THE ISSUE.

Once the woman had Joab's ear, the first thing she did wasn't to accuse, but to clarify. Verses 18-19 say, "She continued, 'In the past they used to say, "Seek counsel in Abel," and that's how they settled disputes. I am one of the peaceful and faithful in Israel, but you're trying to destroy a city that is like a mother in Israel. Why would you devour the Lord's inheritance?'" (2 Samuel 20:18-19, CSB).

This city was known for wisdom. It drew others to it to help them resolve their issues and she even invokes a term, a mother in Israel, that may have prompted Joab to recall the one person who had previously held that title: Deborah.

Judges 4 introduces Deborah sitting under a tree, available for others to come to her to settle disputes and issues. "Deborah, a prophetess and the wife of Lappidoth, was judging Israel at that time. She would sit under the palm tree of Deborah between Ramah and Bethel in the hill country of Ephraim, and the Israelites went up to her to settle disputes" (Judges 4:4-5, CSB). The reference of being a "mother of Israel" comes following the destruction of Sisera and the Cananites. Joab would've known his history. He would have known the old judges of Israel before the rise of the kings. This phrase alone would've prompted him to recall Deborah and how she looked out for Israel.

The woman at the wall used this title to compare what Deborah did for the Israelites to the role the city of Abel played in offering wisdom, counsel, and protection for the surrounding smaller towns. This point of clarification allows her to speak to the protective side of Joab. He was the leader of the ground troops. He had killed the man who was originally told to recruit men to David's side but had proven to be incompetent. He wasn't a soft, teddy bear of a man. He was battle worn and had already defended his king multiple times, to the point of being responsible for the death of David's son, Absalom. He then called out King David when his mourning of the son who tried to kill him was reflecting badly to the troops who had just defended him and his kingship. Joab was tough but understood strategy. He had to in order to be a competent army commander. The woman at the wall wasn't appealing to his humanity as much as his strategic mind. She explained the role of the city, its value in comparison to the importance of a previous judge of Israel and asked if he really wanted to destroy that in the pursuit of one man.

This allowed Joab to respond in kind. "Never! I would never devour or demolish! That is not the case" (2 Samuel 20:20, CSB). He was then able to offer an explanation to their attempted siege. Clarity matters.

I believe that many disagreements are a result of unmet expectations. I know this to be true in my own life, whether with my husband, children, parents, friends, or co-workers. What begins as an unmet expectation, develops into a frustration, then can then develop into a resentment or offense if unaddressed.

Every Tuesday, our church campus has what we call Community Nights. It's a time that the campus is open, kid's ministry is available, and classes of all kinds are offered. Because a large portion of our attendance on this night are single parent families, we also provide a free dinner before the classes begin. The idea is to build family within the community and provide a safe place to connect, learn, and grow.

There are a lot of moving pieces to the evening and so at the beginning of the semester, we as a team discussed every detail and divided the tasks for the night. Each of us could own a piece of the logistics without feeling overwhelmed with taking care of every detail on our own. Oftentimes, we would help out one another when schedules inevitably shifted or if someone wasn't available that week.

One week, my role included teaching at one of the classes. It was the first time I had taught this particular material, and I wanted to make sure I had plenty of time to run through it and work through any technical difficulties early on to reduce my stress later. Thinking I was planning ahead, I went over to take care of my usual responsibilities for the evening and discovered that none of the other details for setting up the night had been done. Because I was already thinking through what I would be teaching, I found myself frustrated that no one thought to just take care of things, surely knowing that one, it wasn't only my job to take care of them, and two, I had other things going on and needed to focus on them instead. In my frustration, I dragged the box of decorations out and sent a message to our team chat to come help me set up, please–I did at least say please.

The next morning, we had a debrief. At that point, I had realized I was reacting from a place of stress and unmet expectations. Instead of making a big deal out of it, like I wanted to the night before, I simply asked that we reevaluate everyone's roles so we could make sure there weren't pieces falling through the cracks. I was able to clarify my frustration and we were able to work out ways to do better in the future.

Reason calls to reason. If we're able to stay level-headed, it can deescalate a lot of otherwise explosive reactions. But when we find the issues clarified, we also need to be sure that we don't dawdle around about how to resolve the issues. We need to be decisive and take the actions that are needed.

BE DECISIVE IN THE RESOLUTION.

One of my daughters hates making decisions. Part of it stems from her being a people-pleaser, but when asked her opinion or even what she wants for dinner she'll hem and haw before saying, "I don't know! I'm not a decision girl!" While we're continuing to work on that, assuring her that she is certainly allowed–and encouraged–to have her own opinions and express them to us, we laugh when she says this knowing she will only have more decisions to make in the future. Things I know about her: her favorite candy is gum, but she'll accept pretty much any sweet. Given a choice of restaurant, she'll choose wings or steak. She loves going for coffee with me and will happily accept any invitation for girly outings like getting mani-pedis. All of these are mindless decisions and ones she has made abundantly clear. But then there are bigger issues, like when she's upset, and we ask what is bothering her. So often she'll say I don't know or just shrug partially because it may be multiple things and partially because she doesn't want to upset anyone else. In the long run, it works better when we can clearly identify the issue and then make a decisive step towards a resolution.

In 2 Samuel, we find that as soon as the issue was clarified, the wise woman made a decision. "The woman replied to Joab, 'Watch! His head will be thrown over the wall to you.' The woman went to all the people with her wise counsel, and they cut off the head of Sheba son of Bichri and threw it to Joab. So he blew the ram's horn, and they dispersed from the city, each to his own tent. Joab returned to the king in Jerusalem.'" (2 Samuel 20:21-22, CSB).

The life of a wicked man versus the well-being of an entire city. Maybe this wasn't the most difficult decision the wise woman and the city council had to make, but it's less about the actual decision and more about how they made it. So many policies and counsels could be greatly effective if they weren't talked to death. Even things that both sides agree on seem to take forever to be enacted because they have to pull apart every unimportant detail before finally agreeing with what they said when the policy was first introduced.

Do you remember Blockbuster? Depending on your age, you may have no clue what I'm talking about. But before the digital, instantaneous streaming age of Netflix, Prime Video, Apple TV, and Disney+ was the movie rental store. My family would love to have pizza and movie nights and for reasons that are completely unknown to me still to this day, we would often send the two people who were the worst at actually making a decision to go pick out the movie: me and my dad. We would walk through the rows, looking at the newest releases then wander over to the classics. We'd joke about getting some ridiculous film, knowing my mom would despise it, but of course not actually choosing that one. We might actually make a decision only to discover that there weren't any copies of that movie left. Very often, we left empty handed, unable to make a simple decision and would instead watch one of the movies we already owned. The ironic part is that if you look at all of the components of my personality—Meyers Briggs, StrengthsFinder, Enneagram, etc.– you would think that I would be a decision-making master.

While choosing what movie to watch isn't life or death, being able to make a decision is an important component to battling the enemy. Joshua commanded the Israelites, "...choose this day whom you will serve, whether the gods your fathers served in the region beyond the River, or the gods of the Amorites in whose land you dwell. But as for me and my house, we will serve the Lord" (Joshua 24:15, ESV).

Before anything else, we need to definitively decide which side of the battle we're on. The world around us lives in the idea of relativism. They like to say things like hold to your truth–as if there can be multiple truths. Here is the truth from Jesus' own mouth: "I am the way, the truth, and the life. No one comes to the Father except through me" (John 14:6, CSB). He's the only way to the Father. He is the only truth, but we have been given the choice to accept Him or to reject Him. If we choose to reject Jesus as the only truth, that doesn't somehow give us the ability to construct our own truths. It simply means that we are unwilling to acknowledge His sacrifice and surrender ourselves to His authority.

I know that sounds abrupt and harsh. I know it sounds judgmental, but please understand that's not my intention. My heart in being direct is to clarify any wavering ideas that go against what the Bible tells us. Part of being able to make decisive resolutions is to have a clear understanding of the information, as we previously discussed. For Christians, that begins with a clear understanding of the Gospel of Jesus Christ. He is our beginning and end. He is the one who came and made a way for us. His response in John 14 came as an answer to Thomas just prior to the crucifixion. Jesus had prepared a special time with His closest friends. They were to share one final Passover meal together and at this time, Jesus was sharing His final thoughts with them, knowing it was one of the last conversations He would have with them before He died. He reminded them that this was necessary; that He was going ahead to prepare a place for them in heaven. Thomas asked how they would know the way if they didn't know where Jesus was going. Jesus responded that He was the way. When we look to Jesus we can see where to go and what direction to take.

Isaiah 30:20-21 says, "The Lord will give you meager bread and water during oppression, but your Teacher will not hide any longer. Your eyes will see your Teacher, and whenever you turn to the right or to the left, your ears will hear this command behind you: 'This is the way. Walk in it.'"

There will be trials; there will be opposition. There will be difficult decisions that make us question who we are, who God made us to be, what is going on, maybe even questioning God a little. That's okay! It may come as a surprise, but God doesn't mind the questions–just be ready for the answer.

Let's consider for a moment the tale of Job. The poor guy was upstanding to the point that Satan accused him of only honoring God because of the blessings God had given him. In response to that accusation God allowed Satan to test Job. He lost everything except his own life and still Job did not curse God–but he did question Him. Job questioned why he was still alive. He questioned why all of this would befall him, but in the midst of his suffering there was a moment when he recognized the sovereignty of God. "But as for me, I know that my Redeemer lives, and he will stand upon the earth at last. And after my body has decayed, yet in my body I will see God! I will see him for myself. Yes, I will see him with my own eyes. I am overwhelmed at the thought!" (Job 19:25-27, NLT).

He knew that even if he were to lose his life, God is alive and well. God is in control, even when circumstances are out of our control. I've recently become aware that control is one of my saboteurs. Saboteurs are those things inside ourselves that work against us. Things that in smaller amounts are extremely beneficial inhibit us when they're pushed too far. Control is a big one for me.

I plan and organize to maintain control. I tap into my God-given strengths of strategy and responsibility to maintain a grip on what's going on and work to predict any possible outcomes of situations. I take on more roles that should instead be delegated because if I'm in charge of it, I will be able to control the outcome and details that someone else may miss. It's a good thing that has gone too far. And there are so many circumstances that are outside of my control.

I couldn't control the car that ran the red light that nearly killed my daughter and injured my other children. I couldn't control the lack of sales on my first book. I couldn't control the way some of the men in the church responded to me in my desire to lead and teach. I couldn't control how my ex-boyfriend decided to speak to me in his own brokenness. I couldn't control whether my extended family designated favorites among my cousins and me.

We can't control the families we're born into. We can't control other people's responses or reactions. There is so much that we can't control but we serve a God who is always in control. We see this in God's response to Job:

Then the LORD answered Job from the whirlwind. He said: "Who is this who obscures my counsel with ignorant words? Get ready to answer me like a man; when I question you, you will inform me. Where were you when I established the earth? Tell me, if you have understanding. Who fixed its dimensions? Certainly, you know! Who stretched a measuring line across it? What supports its foundations? Or who laid its cornerstone while the morning stars sang together, and all the sons of God shouted for joy?" (Job 38:1-7, CSB).

God continues for another 121 verses. He makes it abundantly clear who He is, what He's done, and that, certainly, He is in control. Proverbs 3:5-6 says, "Trust in the Lord with all your heart, and do not rely on your own understanding; in all your ways know him, and he will make your paths straight" (CSB). This was the first verse I remember memorizing, but it took me years to fully understand the beautiful simplicity of this truth.

My desire for control is a representation of relying on my own understanding. The word "know" in this verse is a primitive root word: *yada*. While the literal definition is indeed, "to know," there are places where it means so much more than to have some knowledge of. In Genesis this is the word used when Adam and Eve ate of the fruit and they *knew* they were naked. They had an understanding about what God had been protecting them from once they were introduced to the idea of shame. This is also the word used when it says that Adam *knew* Eve and she became pregnant. Here it takes this idea of knowing and deepens the level of intimacy.

When we *know* God in all our ways, we're transitioning beyond a surface level. We move beyond simply having information about Him, but instead allow Him to open our eyes to the intimate details of who He is. When we look to Him for each area of our lives, leaning fully into the truth of who He is, we can trust that His guidance will be in our best interest. He may allow certain circumstances to try us, but ultimately, they are opportunities for us to grow and then glorify Him.

We can trust His direction and the more we stay attuned to that voice telling us "turn to the right or left" (Isaiah 30:21), the more ready we will be to be decisive in the resolutions before us. We'll be able to absorb the information given and be confident in our decisions. God has given us this incredible ability to think and reason, but He wants us to do it in coordination with Him and His guidance. So whether we're having to take on a vicious battle wrought with deception or simply pick out the movie for family movie night, we can be assured that God is with us and will happily grant us wisdom in each and every situation if we are simply willing to ask.

CHAPTER NINE
CHANGE THE
NARRATIVE
THE DAUGHTERS OF
ZELOPHEHAD | NUMBERS 27

Like many families, for large meals–like Thanksgiving or Christmas–my extended family would always designate a kids' table set apart from the main table where all the adults sat. The main table had the full, proper setting including the nice china, silver flatware, and crystal wine glasses. It included the cloth napkins and of course some form of centerpiece. Then there was the kids' table. While we did often have "real" plates, they would be the heavier, every-day, ceramic plates. Sometimes it was the low center table in the living room, sometimes it was a folding card table that was set up away from where the adults were eating. It was separate not in a way of honoring, but rather designating an established hierarchy.

I don't actually have a problem with the ever-common kids' table. Often it was the most fun and interesting place to be. There was certainly less stress over proper manners and only polite conversation. My cousins and I would reconnect and joke about whatever game we had been playing since the day began. What I find interesting and rather sad is that there are still people who treat women in this same manner. They are relegated to the unofficial table, not seen as equal or mature enough to hold their own in the discussions being had. If they were given a seat at the table, it would lead to disaster or at the very least the shattering of centuries-long traditions.

Sometimes I wonder if God had the stories in the Bible recorded in such a way that there were some accounts that would be obvious to us but then included others just to see if we were really paying attention to all His word. There's one such story recorded in Numbers 27. The book of Numbers begins with a census–hence the name. While having a tedious start, it transitions into a continuation of the telling of the Israelites in the desert, including when they actually make it to the promised land, send in the twelve spies, ten of which got scared, and then had to deal with the consequences of not trusting God which resulted in none of those recorded on that original census (basically anyone aged 20 and older) able to enter the promised land. Just like they continually bemoaned, they would die in the desert never experiencing the blessings God had for them.

But in chapter 26, there is a second census taken following a massive plague (again a consequence for bad choices; this time for allowing Moabite women to draw the Israelite men into an orgy). This census was to divide the inheritance of land among the tribes. It gets to the sons of Joseph by clans through Manasseh and lists the descendants of Gilead: Iezar, Helek, Asriel, Shechem, Shemida, Hepher, and Zelophehad. Then verse 34 says, "Zelophehad son of Hepher had no sons, only daughters. Their names were Mahlah, Noah, Hoglah, Milcah, and Tirzah" (Numbers 26:34, MSG). At this moment, it feels almost like a throw away. Why are the daughters mentioned? Why bother when it just continues with the completion of the clans of Manasseh, which numbered 52,700, and moves on to Ephraim's clans? But come chapter 27, the daughters of Zelophehad show back up and go against what so many decided was the norm for women in that day.

It doesn't give us any more information at the time, but it does lead us to begin to wonder why this detail was given. This has been one of the most interesting ways for me to dig into scripture. Ask why. Begin to look for the parallels. My church's pastor often says, "You can't point to something in the New Testament that I can't also find in the Old." The Bible is a complete story with connecting plot lines from beginning to end. So why were these daughters listed? Because God wanted to remind us that He sees us and we as His daughters have a seat at the table as well. As ezer-warriors, we are equally called to participate in the work of God. He sees us as valuable, not secondary, and wants our voices to be part of the conversation. As we continue on I hope that this is both encouraging and challenging. I don't believe that God is calling all of His daughters to completely change their demeanors and take on a personality that is not their own, but at the same time, there will be circumstances in our lives that will require us to press beyond what we think we're capable of. If you are naturally soft-spoken or incredibly reserved, some of the things I'm proposing may push you more than others. Likewise, if you are naturally rather boisterous and typically outspoken, the challenge may come in learning how to approach some of these characteristics with humility, especially when you know you're right or when it is toward someone who has spoken down to you in the past. Arrogance will never win you favors in the court of heaven. Sayings like "You capture more flies with honey than with vinegar" exist for a reason. We can stand firm on the word of God and still have a humble heart. But be careful you don't use that as an excuse to remain silent. When we see things that are wrong, we are to call it out and bring attention to the issues.

CALL IT OUT.

Numbers 27 begins saying,

The daughters of Zelophehad approached; Zelophehad was the son of Hepher, son of Gilead, son of Machir, son of Manasseh from the clans of Manasseh, the son of Joseph. These were the names of his daughters: Mahlah, Noah, Hoglah, Milcah, and Tirzah. They stood before Moses, the priest Eleazar, the leaders, and the entire community at the entrance to the tent of meeting and said, "Our father died in the wilderness, but he was not among Korah's followers, who gathered together against the Lord. Instead, he died because of his own sin, and he had no sons. Why should the name of our father be taken away from his clan? Since he had no son, give us property among our father's brothers" (Number 27:1-4, CSB).

These five women bring their case to the forefront. They approached the table where they were not readily welcomed and challenged the status quo. Just like when we talked about the woman at the wall recognizing authority, the daughters of Zelophehad didn't say the leaders were wrong or that Moses had certainly misunderstood God's directives when he met with Him on the mountain top. Instead, they brought attention to a detail that wasn't specifically addressed in the law that would cause an oversight to honoring one of the descendants of the tribes of Israel.

Confrontation is a tricky topic to tackle. Some take it on too willingly while others avoid it like the plague. There is such a thing as healthy conflict, and it is necessary in all of our relationships.

We are unique and beautifully created in an infinite combination of similarities and differences. When our opinions or understandings vary, it can cause other people to respond negatively. If ignored, conflict doesn't just disappear–it grows. It festers and becomes more painful than if it had been addressed right away.

During a prayer time at work one week, one of the pastors compared challenging circumstances to a physical injury. Some injuries can be addressed with a little antibacterial ointment and a band-aid. Others, like a broken bone, will hurt to reset, but that pain and discomfort is necessary to allow for proper healing. Then you have those injuries that have been ignored. What may have started as an innocuous cut, if it was never cleaned out, becomes a larger problem once the germs have begun to wreak havoc and infection has set in. These require intense cleaning, sometimes literal scrubbing, to clear out and remove the infection before you can begin to bandage them. Conflict mirrors this as well. Some issues are minor and just need a little patch job to clarify a misunderstood tone or use of the wrong wording. Other times, that conflict will trigger deeper hurts. To address these, it may require going in to reset the deeper hurt before the current conflict can be dealt with. Finally, there are those conflicts that have been ignored over and over again. Think of these like the gangrene of relationships. They stink and literally rot us from the inside out. There are times that the only solution is to completely amputate the situation or see the death of a relationship.

We can't just avoid difficult conversations, no matter how uncomfortable they may make us. And the enemy loves to stir up conflict and misunderstandings. Disunity is his playground. Disunity causes hurts and offenses. It deceives us into thinking that we have to completely agree to see unity and restitution. That's a lie. We don't actually have to agree about things to have unity. We can have different opinions but be unified in our spirits. The Spirit isn't limited to a single perspective or an unintentional bias. If issues aren't a heaven-or-hell issue, a difference in opinion is possible while still remaining in unity.

SKULL CRUSHERS

I have a co-worker who has a very different personality than mine. She wants to help and empower volunteers, but I sometimes feel like she misses pieces that I view as important details. How we approach projects and working with volunteers is different–neither is inherently right nor wrong. One day, I overheard a discussion she was having with a volunteer regarding some of the ways we structure groups within the organization. Having recently addressed this with other volunteers, I spoke up–thinking I was helping and knowing I had already done a lot of work to address this particular issue. She responded that she would take it into consideration and then continued with her previous train of thought.

I perceived her response–which she meant in kindness–as a brush-off and it triggered places inside of me that had been previously ignored. What she didn't know at the time was that I had emotional injuries from times that other co-workers had brushed off my ideas as not important or worth their consideration and her response mirrored theirs when they were simply trying to placate me. My interjection–which I meant to be helpful and hopefully save her some work–was received as intruding and not viewing her as competent in her role.

We were both hurt in this interaction because we didn't understand where the other person was coming from. Since that time, I've made an intentional decision to get to know her better. I want to understand her heart so that I can better support her without triggering a previous hurt. Likewise, I want to be better aware of my own triggers so that I can own up to them when they happen.

When I ignored the situation, it led to more annoyances and more frustrations between the two of us. But as we talked and sought to truly hear one another's heart and intent, we have been able to become a more unified team. We still often approach projects differently, but again a difference in opinion doesn't necessarily mean we aren't unified. When our spirits are humbled to the guidance of the Father, we're able to see it as simply what it is: a difference in approaches that allows our team to be better because we can see multiple perspectives of each project we work on together.

Disunity doesn't just happen from the words we say, sometimes it grows from the words we don't say. America has seen an uprising in media coverage surrounding racial tension. There is still debate on whether the occurrences themselves are increasing or if there is simply more coverage of them. Much of the hurt developed between friends and neighbors when, in light of horrific situations, many remained silent. Even with differing opinions on how to address the situations, we can still speak out for justice. We can recognize when something is wrong and we can be willing to have conversations–to allow those who feel invisible to be both seen and heard.

While we need to be cognizant about those things that are merely opinion or innate biases, we as believers are called to call out injustices. We as warriors need to intimately know God's word so that we can know what His word says about issues. This has been a warning from God since the beginning. The purpose of the law was to set apart His chosen people from the other peoples in the lands they were sojourning to. Today we are called to be set apart, or sanctified. We are called to look and act differently from those who don't know Jesus. The prophet Isaiah warned against the coming destruction of the kingdom of Judah when he said, "Woe to those who call evil good and good evil, who substitute darkness for light and light for darkness, who substitute bitter for sweet and sweet for bitter...who acquit the guilty for a bribe and deprive the innocent of justice" (Isaiah 5:20, 23 CSB).

Warriors for God will look and act differently than the general public. We will allow God's word to guide our sense of justice and we will call out those things that we know are wrong. We will strive for unity and seek resolution within our conflicts with others. And we do it together.

The daughters of Zelophehad were probably like most sisters and argued among one another. There were likely occasional power plays or the random acting out in defiance. My sister and I are very typical first- and second-born. Growing up, my sister would be more cautious and has always been more of a people-pleaser. I, on the other hand, would push limits and lived a little more chaotically because of it. As we both have grown up and matured in ourselves and in our relationship with one another, we've established a precedent when issues come up. If there is something going on within the family, we'll call and discuss it amongst ourselves. We don't always agree but will come to a common ground in how we want to address it to anyone else. Before approaching others, we become a completely unified front. I have her back and I know she has mine.

Have you ever seen a pride of lionesses hunt? As a pride, they surround the prey. They use teamwork to guide the prey where they need it to ultimately capture it. They don't do it by singling out one of the lionesses or by attacking one another. They are unified and in doing so are extremely efficient.

Ladies, we are each other's pride. We are lionesses, especially designed to be efficient and effective when we work together. When we support one another, we're stronger. When we come together and present a single idea, it is better received and more clearly heard. When we use our voices to lift one another up, disunity melts away leaving a powerful, confident group of warriors. As we begin walking confidently in this, we will be fully equipped to then claim the territory God has set aside for us.

CLAIM YOUR TERRITORY.

Capture the flag was always a popular game to play in student ministry. Both when I was growing up and when I served as a volunteer in my early twenties, it was a standard go-to activity. Hide your flag somewhere within your territory, then have at least one person guarding it while the others venture into enemy land to attempt to find and capture their flag for all of the glory and bragging rights. Because the line between territories was usually somewhat ambiguous, it could lead to some contention when the enemy flag passed from one side to the other. Was it a clear victory or were they stopped before making it?

Throughout the world, country lines have changed and shifted with every war, colonization, and political agreement over the ages. One of my favorite classes in college was a study in Palestinian and Israeli relations. This was at a public university and so taught from a secular standpoint. Even so, the professor did a remarkable job at presenting the information neutrally. The class itself, however, was divided between the two nations. In particular, there was one girl who sat in front of me who was Jewish. Every class she would leave on the phone with her dad, occasionally in tears over the focus of the lecture. The battles that raged between the Israelites and the people who are now known as Palestinians are the same in secular history as found in the histories in the Bible.

God gave Abraham the land known as Canaan but then they left for years, allowing time for other people groups to occupy it. The Philistines, the Ammonites, and the Hittites–among others–all called this land home. They followed abhorrent practices including but not limited to child sacrifice, brutal religious practices that were obscenely sexual in unnatural and often violent ways, justice that wasn't actually justice but the king's manner of killing anyone who disagreed or annoyed him, slavery, brutality, and more. God wanted more for His people. By clearing out those whose hearts were set against the things of God, He was able to give His people a territory where they could instead establish practices that honored and provided true justice and mercy. The Israelites were tasked with showing the benefits of honoring God and the blessings that resulted from it. They were to show the world that there was a better way of doing things. In fact, this is what the early church later began to accomplish as they were the one's who set the precedent for sexual morality and allowing women to be active members of the faith. Their actions were completely countercultural and influenced the world around them so that in time, it became more of the social norm.

To accomplish this great shift in culture, the Israelites had to take back the territory they previously lost. They had to wage war against severely violent people. They had to listen to God's guidance in the condition of the hearts of those people groups they were battling. The Bible tells us that the Israelites were to annihilate the people, leaving no one alive. We know this wasn't done by the fact that these same people groups kept creeping back up into the story and conflicts arose against them. There are two sides to this: one side was disobedience on the Israelites' part to not address a certain leader and the other side is hyperbole. Ancient texts are filled with exaggerations when it comes to the retelling of wars and battles. In this instance, God wasn't tasking them to go and literally kill every man, woman, and child without restraint. They were to take care of the leadership and those who adamantly opposed God. Like in Egypt, this was less about the persons and more about clearing out the false gods.

My husband and I had been talking about starting a garden for years. We always wanted the option of fresh produce but despite being the daughter of a farmer, I notoriously kill plants. As our kids have gotten older, the idea resurfaced more often to be utilized as lessons for them in both farming, horticulture, and basic responsibility. For Mother's Day 2021, my husband finally went and bought materials to set up the garden space. We determined where we were going to put everything but for whatever reason, the person working at the garden center told my husband he didn't need anything under the soil to prevent weeds and grass from growing through.

Several months after placing the raised border, pouring in the dirt, and planting our small selection of starter vegetables, I can safely tell you that yes, we did need that sheet. But even more so, we needed to have completely cleared out all the grass even before the border was established. It's not impossible for my little plants to grow, but I have a lot more work to keep the weeds cleared out so they don't strangle the vegetables I chose to plant in that ground. It isn't impossible for them to grow, but it is much harder for them to flourish.

God has given each of us a territory. He may ask us to cultivate the land. Breaking down anything that was previously established and clearing out the overgrowth. This is hard work. It requires physical stamina and perseverance. We need to be attentive that we are clearing those things that hinder but not disrupt any new life or dreams that are starting to peek through. Perhaps it was already previously cleared out and now needs us to care and maintain that territory. This takes dedication and consistency. It requires responsibility to know when to water and when the area needs added sustenance. Discernment and knowledge from God is vital in times like this. But no matter what the condition of the territory before you, we must fully recognize and accept the fact that yes, God gives us the territories, but we are only conduits for God's work. We care for what is before us and are faithful, but it is God alone who causes growth to happen. Our role is absolutely vital, but we are neither the beginning or the end. It's not for our glory that we claim this territory, but what God wants to do in and through us.

"So give us an inheritance among our father's relatives" (Numbers 27:4, MSG). Zelophehad's daughters show up and stake a claim to what rightfully belongs to their family. They aren't making complaints that they've been treated unfairly or playing victim that their father has died and so there is no one to look out for them. They are standing up for what they know is right and what they understand to be the true heart of God for His people. This may not be the ambiguous territory lines like in capturing the flag, but it is setting a new precedent.

Isaiah 54 says, "'Rejoice, childless one, who did not give birth; burst into song and shout, you who have not been in labor! For the children of the desolate one will be more than the children of the married woman,' says the Lord. 'Enlarge the site of your tent, and let your tent curtains be stretched out; do not hold back; lengthen your ropes, and drive your pegs deep. For you will spread out to right and to the left, and your descendants will dispossess nations and inhabit the desolate cities'" (Isaiah 54:1-3, CSB).

God had instructed the Israelites to take hold of the territory He had for them for more than just the physical land. Ancient history through the time of the early church shows us that you were born into your religion. The culture you grew up in, the family who birthed you, and the land you called home was all part of the faith you would have grown up knowing. Christianity changed that. Jesus changed that. The blood of Jesus transcended beyond familial lines. It seeped into the very structure of who and what we all are. Rather than being told by culture what to believe, Jesus made a way for us to be adopted into a new family–His family.

The territory that the daughters of Zelophehad claimed may have been literal, but for the daughters of God today, we are standing to claim spiritual territory. The blood of Jesus created a way for it to happen but that doesn't mean that He doesn't have anything for us to do. The verses in Isaiah give instruction for preparation. Isaiah spoke to the heart of Israel in promising that God would keep His promise made long ago to Noah that He wouldn't wipe out the entire earth. The land that they were about to inhabit in Numbers and Joshua is the same land that they later lost in Kings and Chronicles, and the same land they returned to at Cyrus' decree in Ezra. It was still a physical representation of what God was going to accomplish in the spiritual through Jesus.

Through the work and sacrifice of Jesus, that territory is no longer limited to a certain section of dirt along the Mediterranean Sea. It has "spread out to the right and to the left." The desolate cities are not only broken-down buildings but broken hearts. The cultivation that God places before us extends into the hearts and minds of the people around us.

What territory has God given you? It begins at home. For me that includes my husband and children. How I steward that territory affects how efficient I can be at other territories. God graciously extends that reach every time I have an opportunity to teach or through writing. Again, I am simply the tool being used. I am not the one who determines the outcome or the growth. We are not responsible for changing people's hearts. We are responsible to reach out to those around us with the love of Jesus. We are responsible for caring for those within our territories. We are responsible for stepping out when God calls us, but He is the one who does the work. He is the one who receives (and deserves) the glory. We are simply called to hear Him, believe what He says to be true, and obey Him and all that He's called us to do. Our obedience creates ripples in the world around us. Just as the Israelites were supposed to show the surrounding nations a different manner of governing, and just as the early church showed the surrounding cultures a different standard of morality, we too are called to change the world around us. By walking out in obedience to God and living fully in His love, we will drastically change the rules that before we always thought to be concrete.

CHANGE THE RULES.

"God ruled: 'Zelophehad's daughters are right. Give them land as an inheritance among their father's relatives. Give them their father's inheritance. ...Then tell the people...This is the standard procedure for the People of Israel, as commanded by God through Moses'" (Numbers 27:6-11, MSG).

When the sisters united together, called out the injustice, and claimed the territory the God had set aside for them, they didn't simply get what they wanted, but they established a new standard for all of the People of Israel. Daughters were able to inherit the land where all other surrounding cultures saw their daughters as nothing more than property to be traded for wealth or prestige.

God sees His daughters. He hears the cries of our hearts as we face unfair standards that put limits against us but not men. He has captured every tear that has fallen and has echoed the frustration that radiated from our very core. Inequality and division between His sons and daughters is not from Him. God is love and mercy and justice. He doesn't just have those traits; those characteristics are who He is–and He can't change because He is also infinite and everlasting.

What does that mean for us? That means that God has so much more for you than you could ever think, dream, or imagine. It means that when there is someone who tells you that you can't do something you heard God calling you to do, they are not speaking on behalf of God. If your Father gives you a dream or a calling, then He will help you accomplish it. We are given incredible purpose, but we have to have enough faith to face the opposition before us. Do we actually believe that God will complete the work He began in us (Philippians 1:6)? Do we believe that God has a plan for us filled with a great future and hope (Jeremiah 29:11)?

For almost two years, I worked as a ministry coordinator for the student ministry at the church we attended. My role was to ensure the activities and topics we were doing within the ministry were reaching our girls as well as the boys. Prior to coming on board, we had started to see great growth in the numbers of students attending on a weekly basis. Unfortunately, the vast majority of that growth was in boys. The girls were still attending, but the numbers for them were stagnant. I was given the freedom to work closely with recruiting new female leaders, establishing small groups for our girls, and even executing a girls-only retreat each year. I loved this job. I loved working with the teenagers and seeing them grow in their faith. I loved having an opportunity to teach at the retreat and to begin to discover my own calling of speaking at the same time.

The goal for this position was to prove its need to our church elders. I wanted to show that we needed to diversify the staff to better reach not only the young men in our communities, but the young women. I wanted them to understand that there were things that I could accomplish as a woman that our young male student pastor and his even younger male interns missed, even with the best of intentions.

I was unsuccessful in this particular goal, and it hurt for a very long time. We moved shortly after this, but I continued to carry the hurt for a couple more years. In the time following, I began to see exponential growth in my own faith. I gained a clearer understanding of the prophetic and was able to learn at the feet of some incredible female leaders. I experienced first-hand what it looked like for men and women to serve in the church together. And over time, that hurt I carried was healed. Since then, that same young male student pastor has gone on to start his own church and has a much more balanced approach to women in church leadership. He's even asked my opinion on dealing with those who oppose women teaching from the platform on the weekends. He likely would have come to this place without my influence, as he has an incredibly strong wife, mother, and sister to help influence him as well, but there's also the possibility that my insistence on wanting to teach and wanting my voice heard helped guide him to a place of greater understanding. Perhaps not, but the point is that I was faithful in the things to which God called me.

I have had to intentionally offer back my dreams to God, but with the knowledge that if it is truly from Him, He will only bless my open-handed offering. When God clarifies our callings, it isn't something to be hoarded. Instead, it's with the understanding that it may be for a season. When God asks you to shift or to give up one of those dreams, know that He isn't doing it to take from you or to be mean. He's doing it because He has something even better for you.

The actions that we take today will later affect our daughters and nieces. The steps that I take to help bring understanding to the church on the role of women will affect the roles that will be readily open to my daughters and my niece. This isn't activism, but a lifestyle. This is about shifting our perspective to reflect the heart of our Father. When we begin to look more like Him, others notice. We stand out. We can make waves without causing others to capsize under our influence.

In mid-December 1867, Amy Carmichael was born in Northern Ireland. Raised by Christian parents, she developed a heart for the disadvantaged from an early age. She would regularly bring girls who worked in the mills to church, but not everyone welcomed them. So instead of bending to the expectations of others, Amy purchased a tin building to be a meeting place for these girls. What she originally called Welcome Hall is still there today, known as Welcome Evangelical Church in Belfast.[34]

Later, she responded to a call to serve as a missionary in Japan. Due to health issues, she moved to China but ultimately ended up in Southern India. While serving there, Amy discovered that little girls were being "offered" to Hindu temples to be "married to the gods," which just meant that they became temple prostitutes. In response, she created a safe place to bring those girls, and later boys, who were trafficked. The hostel grew to also become a hospital and eventually helped influence the change of laws to help protect children from the abuse.

She dedicated 56 years to live alongside those she ministered to in Dohnavur, India. The Dohnavur Fellowship exists still today and "works toward holistic development, running projects across the areas of Child Development, Education, Health Care, Community Development and the Conservation of Nature."[35]

She didn't demand attention and she isn't someone of whom many are aware, but her heart for the disadvantaged and abused influenced others such as Jim and Elisabeth Elliot—the famous missionaries to Ecuador. By simply doing as God called her, she was able to establish two different places for people to be welcomed in and learn about the love of God, no matter what their background is.

Changing the rules doesn't have to be obstinate or disrespectful. It doesn't have to undermine anyone or lead to revolts. Sometimes, the most influential manner of change is the most subtle. As we journey

---

[34] https://www.evangelical-times.org/articles/historical/the-life-and-legacy-of-amy-carmichael/. Accessed 12/2/2021.

[35] https://dohnavurfellowship.org/. Accessed 12/2/2021.

on, it's clear that there are an infinite number of ways to change the world. God will use those things that you are naturally gifted in as well as put you into situations that are intentionally more than you can handle on your own because He wants you to depend on Him. He might bring you to a place where your heart breaks for a situation you either see or experience firsthand, allowing your test to become your testimony. Are we willing to trust Him in these times? Are we willing to surrender our own agendas to allow God to be the one who determines what rules are going to change? When we allow His discretion to dictate our steps, we will begin to see mountains of injustice and disunity crumble. If we are obedient to His call, the narrative will begin to reflect the truth of His love for all His children and lives will be forever changed for the Kingdom of God.

CHAPTER TEN
MORE THAN JUST A CHARACTER TRAIT
THE SHUNAMMITE WOMAN |
2 KINGS 4:8-37

In most Biblical narrative (really any historical narrative) women are listed as the wife of so-and-so, recognizing them by whomever their husbands happen to be. There are a few exceptions to this and one is found in the beginning of 2 Kings. The history of the Israelites following Solomon until the downfall of both the kingdoms of Israel and Judah can be found in Kings and Chronicles. Like I mentioned previously, the difference in the two is more a matter of perspective based on when they were recorded (during captivity or after their subsequent freedom). This story is about an unnamed woman caring for the prophet Elisha.

The prophets held enormous influence as they were the physical representation of God's word and Spirit and would be sought after to advise the kings, even those who didn't actively honor God during their reigns. They would travel throughout the territories as God led them and likely traveled a familiar route–traversing through the same towns many times over the years. Being that Elisha served

Elijah before he was taken up to heaven in the chariot, Elisha was a common face and incredibly well known and respected. One of the cities Elisha traveled through was the city of Shunem. This area was traditionally part of the tribe of Issachar. If we go back to 1 Chronicles, when the land was first divided, we see that this tribe was known as "mighty men of valor" (1 Chronicles 7).

Why does any of this history matter for the context of our story? I believe by understanding the roles that each person played, we can better appreciate what this woman accomplished and how the known trait of the tribe of Issachar was in the heart of this unnamed woman, something that is in the heart of each of us today.

2 Kings 4:8 says, "One day Elisha went to Shunem. A prominent woman who lived there persuaded him to eat some food. So whenever he passed by, he stopped there to eat." Part of me wants to make a joke that she must've been a great cook, or something along those lines. But I believe there was more to it than a full belly. The first thing we learn about her is that she was considered prominent; some versions describe her as a great woman. She was well known and likely highly respected for her to take on the role of caring for the man of God.

Being "nice" has become a vanilla trait. What I mean is that while it's good, there's nothing inherently special or unique about it. It doesn't set us apart or allow us to stand out. Consider the response, "Well, isn't that nice." Everyone appreciates it but it's just as readily ignored. Ironically, one of the synonyms for nice is subtle. A surface level evaluation of this verse would deem the Shunammite woman was "nice." She did what was expected for someone in her role and even though we get a little more knowledge in that she was a prominent member of the town, it's still just vanilla.

I try to be nice, but I don't believe that it is a characteristic that most would list when describing me. It's not that I'm not nice, but I don't go out of my way in the ways that would be tied to that particular descriptive. Direct, driven, maybe even helpful. Even when thinking of people I would choose to describe as genuinely nice, I'd be more inclined to choose descriptives like gentle, kind, or sweet–not nice. I feel like some might read this passage and just see the woman as being nice. Travelers in this age would've been dependent on the generosity of others if they had to stop on their journeys. A drink or a meal would've been customary, but what we very quickly learn about this woman is that she didn't just accept the expected role of hostess for a meal but saw that this man of God was weary and knew she could do something about it.

SHOW INITIATIVE.

There are times when we feel stuck in our current roles. Whether by the confines of others or of our making, a wall has been constructed around what we do and what we might be able to do–effectively cutting off the potential that used to flow like wild vines around the dreams of our hearts. Ask yourself this question: if you could do anything, be anything, what would you do? Ask children this same question and the sky isn't even the limit. They don't understand constructs like money and education that ultimately limit the truth of possibility. They don't even understand why it simply isn't possible to be a surgeon, construction worker, trapeze artist, and parent all at the same time. It's why you can also get answers like a princess or Spider-Man.

Reality is a brutal beast that we all face at some point or another–some of us much sooner than others. But a dose of reality isn't the problem. The problem is that we continue to shrink the options well beyond what reality says until we can't hardly dream at all. But what would happen if we broke down some of those walls? What if we allowed ourselves to look at our passions and rather than immediately see why they are impossible, we instead focused on how we could take some initiative in using those passions to advance the kingdom and solve some of the problems that plague our world?

The Shunammite woman may have had more resources than other people in the town, but we don't know that for certain. We know she invited Elisha to eat at their table and each time he came through, he chose to return. We know she saw the burden Elisha was carrying and rather than shuffling her feet and wringing her hands about it, she told her husband her idea.

"Then she said to her husband, 'I know that the one who often passes by here is a holy man of God, so let's make a small, walled-in upper room and put a bed, a table, a chair, and a lamp there for him. Whenever he comes, he can stay there'" (2 Kings 4:9-10, CSB). I'll go out on a limb here and assume her husband agreed to her idea since the next verse tells us about an interaction with Elisha while he was in the suggested upstairs room.

It's easy to write off ideas, even good ideas. It's easy to presume that someone else will meet the need that we see. But here's the thing, God may have brought that problem directly to you because He wants you to solve it. Perhaps that challenge that is burdening your heart is there because you are meant to do something about it. In 2011, a man named Michael Hirsch began an organization in Norman, Oklahoma, with the focus to start an afterschool program designed for middle school students. Since then, Loveworks Leadership Inc. has been "committed to empowering youth to become leaders by giving every student an opportunity to lead."[36] I had the privilege of seeing some of the program firsthand when a group of us went up to meet with Michael and his team at

---

[36] https://www.loveworksleadership.org/about/. Accessed 12/2/2021.

Loveworks. What I saw were kids able to learn hands-on about different areas that interest them. I saw middle schoolers challenged to present their ideas with clarity and competency. I saw teams of adults serving these kids, showing them that they are loved and that they matter. I saw a successful organization that has reached the lives of over 12,000 students and continues to make headway as some of these kids learn how to start and run their own businesses.[37] Loveworks Leadership Inc. exists because one man saw someplace he could make a difference and was obedient to step out in faith.

Stepping out in faith is half of the battle. When we sit back and wait, there is a chance that we will miss out not only on an opportunity to be an active participant in the work God is doing, but in receiving an incredible blessing as well.

SECURE THE BLESSING.

The initiative of the Shunammite woman led to creating a consistent place where Elisha could be refreshed. She saw the physical needs of a man who was working to provide for the people's spiritual needs. This action led to a tremendous outpouring of thanks from Elisha in the form of the child she secretly desired.

One day he came there and stopped at the upstairs room to lie down. He ordered his attendant Gehazi, "Call this Shunammite woman." So he called her and she stood before him.

Then he said to Gehazi, "Say to her, 'Look, you've gone to all this trouble for us. What can we do for you? Can we speak on your behalf to the king or to the commander of the army?'"

---

[37] Two of the businesses you can purchase products from are Wrist World (wrist.world) and Real Kitchen Salsa (real.kitchen)

She answered, "I am living among my own people."

So he asked, "Then what should be done for her?"

Gehazi answered, "Well, she has no son, and her husband is old."

"Call her," Elisha said. So Gehazi called her, and she stood in the doorway. Elisha said, "At this time next year you will have a son in your arms."

Then she said, "No, my lord. Man of God, do not lie to your servant."

The woman conceived and gave birth to a son at the same time the following year, as Elisha had promised her (2 Kings 4:11-17, CSB).

God knows the desires of our hearts. Elisha, seeking to honor her, began by offering her a worldly position. For some, this would be the dream. They desire to have notoriety and positional influence. I love her response: "I am living among my own people." Her priorities were different than just climbing a social ladder. She was a woman of valor in her community–well respected and established. She didn't need to have a position among the king's court or a military command. She understood that she was exactly where she needed to be to do the work that God had given her.

Ladies, God has you where you are, at this moment in time, for a specific reason. It's easy to look at those who are seemingly in a dream position, envy what they are able to accomplish, and entirely miss the work that God is doing inside us in our own experiences. Or perhaps this is an exceptionally tough season for you. We learned with Hagar that the wilderness, while so often associated with challenge or even disobedience, is used by God to readily draw us closer to Him. He uses the wilderness to pull us away from distraction so that we can experience Him in new and miraculous ways. Those challenges might be the very thing that bring you to a fresh understanding of God and a blessing for your next season.

I can easily get caught up by looking at people who have the jobs I would love to do but are fifteen years younger than me. I can compare myself to what they have accomplished, to what they get to do. But in doing so, I'll be so busy looking around at others that I miss what God has placed right in front of me. I would miss the conversations I get to have with the ladies that come to the classes I get to teach. I would miss the lessons I have garnered from other leaders and pastors around me, people who graciously pour out their wisdom to me. I would miss so many sweet moments that I have with God as He whispers to my heart and creates this path, allowing me to grow closer to Him.

The Shunammite woman wasn't wanting to advance her position, but she did still have a desire deep in her heart–a child. We're told that her husband was old, which might also insinuate that she, too, was older and no longer able to have children. Despite all the reasons that it wasn't possible, that desire was still there.

Do you have a desire buried deep inside your heart that you think is no longer viable? You see all the reasons why it can't happen. You may even rationalize it to yourself–maybe even to others. But it's still there, the tiniest of sparks, flickering weakly. And in the dark, even the tiniest of sparks can glow brightly.

God revealed that desire to Elisha and with it came a promise of a fulfilled blessing. One year later she held the blessing in the form of a son. Ladies, hold on to the promises of God. That doesn't mean to strangulate them. Nor does it mean to lightly grasp them to the point that they slip through your fingers but hold them and posture them before the Lord. Allow Him to confirm them to you so that when that promise is tested, you can stand firm in full faith. Steadfast faith in your blessing is a mantle of an ezer. The Shunammite woman was truly filled with valor, believing the promise given to her even in the face of the death of that promise.

When we look back at this story in 2 Kings 4, an unknown number of years have passed, and we find the son now old enough to join his father and the harvesters. Something happened and the son's head began to hurt. He was then taken to his mother and while sitting on her lap, he died. Her promise—her deepest desire—died in her arms without warning and without reason.

Despite what must have been severe devastation, she stood up, closed the door, and left to get Elisha. Keep in mind that Elisha represented the voice of God and His Spirit at this time. When everything is going wrong, when our hearts are broken, when the promises appear to have died, are we allowing it to overwhelm us or are we seeking after God?

When I first felt called into speaking and writing, I was scared to seek out opportunities. I would say yes anytime I was asked to teach but taking the initiative to go after those speaking gigs was intimidating. One of the first times I finally put myself out there, I approached a church where I was previously an active volunteer. They knew me, knew what I could do, and yet, I was told no. It was a slammed door in the face of what I thought I was supposed to be doing. I believed this was what God had told me to do and to receive rejection in that area hurt worse than I cared to admit. While I handled it fine on the phone, I allowed the hurt to bury deep into my soul and offense began to take root against the young men who made the decision. It wasn't until a few years later, as I began to find spiritual healing in other areas that God brought me to that place of hurt—revealing it so that He could heal it. What could have been addressed right away, I hid away and allowed to fester. I could have grown and learned from this rejection, knowing that it wasn't God telling me I was wrong in understanding my new calling. I could have taken the opportunity to receive feedback from people I knew. At the very least I could have gone to God immediately rather than curling in on myself, leading to years of doubting myself and the promise from God.

While I pulled away from God when I felt rejection after seeking that speaking opportunity, when we had our car accident in 2016, my immediate response was to go to God and press into His presence and promises. When we were hit, it was as if a pair of mufflers were put over my ears. Everything felt distant, disconnected. People were on the scene right away, helping get my two younger children out of their car seats and attempting to calm their fearful cries. My own exit from the car was slowed by the shattered seatbelt holding me in place. By the time I rounded the back of my car, which had swung around 180 degrees and was now pushed flush against the curb, three men were maneuvering my oldest daughter from the third row after having to break her booster seat to release her. As they gingerly laid her down on the grass, my heart clenched in my chest, cutting off my airways as I breathed, "Jesus, please no!"

My five-year-old was motionless on the grass, looking small and broken—none of us even able to imagine the full extent of the injuries lurking beneath the surface of her neck. My first thought was that I had lost my baby girl. I feared that I would never see her grow and become the woman of God I believed she would be. I felt as though the promise of my firstborn had been stolen from me. But in that moment—and during the long, miraculous journey that followed—I found myself pleading at the feet of Jesus to save my daughter. I found myself pressing into the promise of the meaning of her name—God protects—and asking for miracles I had never seen nor experienced.

The Shunammite woman quickly goes to Elisha. Anyone who asks her along the way, her only response was, "It's all right." She kept her eyes on the one man she knew could change the situation and when she came before him, she fell at his feet and demonstrated that it was in fact not all right, but she believed that it could be.

When she came up to the man of God at the mountain, she clung to his feet. Gehazi came to push her away, but the man of God said, "Leave her alone — she is in severe anguish, and the Lord has hidden it from me. He hasn't told me."

Then she said, "Did I ask my lord for a son? Didn't I say, 'Do not lie to me?'"

So Elisha said to Gehazi, "Tuck your mantle under your belt, take my staff with you, and go. If you meet anyone, don't stop to greet him, and if a man greets you, don't answer him. Then place my staff on the boy's face."

The boy's mother said to Elisha, "As the Lord lives and as you yourself live, I will not leave you." So he got up and followed her (2 Kings 4:27-30, CSB).

She went before the man of God and allowed her vulnerability to show. She pointed to that desire that was given to her first as a promise and then as a blessing. She wasn't willing to just give up and accept that sometimes things happen. In this moment, she understood that her son represented more than just someone to carry on their name and inherit their property. She remembered the faith of Abraham who, "By faith Abraham, when he was tested, offered up Isaac. He received the promises and yet he was offering his one and only son, the one to whom it had been said, Your offspring will be traced through Isaac. He considered God to be able even to raise someone from the dead; therefore, he received him back, figuratively speaking" (Hebrews 11:17-19, CSB).

She may not have willingly offered up her son as Abraham did, but she carried the same faith. And it was in that faith that she was able to secure the blessing by seeking out the one man who could do something about it.

SEEK GOD ABOVE ALL.

When she was looking into the face of her son–her promise–seeing that promise die, she didn't succumb. She didn't melt away and shut down. She went directly to the one who gave her the promise and brought the problem to his feet. Like I previously mentioned, in that time the prophets were the physical representative of God. The woman only spoke to Elisha about her son and she then refused to leave his side. She clung to her promise and equally to the man who represented God to her. Her devotion to seek God above all else led to experiencing the miraculous.

When Elisha got to the house, he discovered the boy lying dead on his bed. So he went in, closed the door behind the two of them, and prayed to the Lord. Then he went up and lay on the boy: he put mouth to mouth, eye to eye, hand to hand. While he bent down over him, the boy's flesh became warm. Elisha got up, went into the house, and paced back and forth. Then he went up and bent down over him again. The boy sneezed seven times and opened his eyes. Elisha called Gehazi and said, "Call the Shunammite woman." He called her and she came. Then Elisha said, "Pick up your son." She came, fell at his feet, and bowed to the ground; she picked up her son and left (2 Kings 4:32-37, CSB).

Today, we don't have to go through someone else to encounter God. He calls all of us to Himself directly. Life and circumstances can clog us up. The realities we face and the heartbreak we feel is real but can sometimes serve to only prevent us from breathing in the Breath of Heaven clearly.

Living first in Florida and then in Texas, I am intimately familiar with seasonal allergies. Every spring and fall, I try my best to preempt the inevitable onslaught of pollen and allergens. I take the necessary supplements and up my intake of orange juice and vegetables that support my immune system. Basically, I do all the things to give my body a fighting chance of remaining gunk-free and able to breathe clearly. Most years, however, there is at least once that the congestion sets in, my head becomes muddled, and my breathing is greatly impaired.

It's then that I pull out the different medication options, from more natural supplements to every antihistamine known. Over the years, I've developed a certain immunity to some of the medications, so I learned to depend on others. Generally, it's just something that must run its course, but there seems to be this one hump to clear before I know I'm on the other side of congested misery. While I might sneeze throughout, at a random, undeterminable point, I will have a ginormous sneeze that is followed by immediate relief. It's as if that one sneeze clears out every obstruction and I'm finally able to breathe.

Elisha, the physical representation of the Spirit of God, got face to face with the boy. Do you remember how God began life in Mankind? "Then the Lord God formed the man out of the dust from the ground and breathed the breath of life into his nostrils, and the man became a living being" (Genesis 2:7, CSB). The presence of God and the Breath of God brought the boy back to life. He sneezed out whatever had blocked him, and life was returned to him.

Ruach is the Hebrew word for spirit. When used as Ruach Elohim it is directly referring to the Spirit of God or the Holy Spirit. It is also translated as wind or breath. It is the Breath of God–the Holy Spirit–that brings us life. It is the Spirit of God that transforms us from merely existing to truly living.

When we seek God above all else in our lives, we readily recognize the congestion created by things in this world. We can see the distractions. We feel the conflict from those areas that are being revealed so that God can heal them. We begin to realize just how blocked off we are from that breath of life–the source that brings healing, freedom, and life. Being able to battle the enemy as an ezer forces us to seek God first. He is the one who provides. He is the one who redeems. He is one who completes us and offers us peace despite our circumstances.

God has equipped His ezers with a multitude of distinctive character traits, much like the woman from Shunem. It's easy to miss, but her faith and actions led her to be included alongside some of the spiritual "greats," as we like to think of them, found in Hebrews 11:35. When we show initiative to honor Him, then fully appreciate the blessings He gives, and seek Him above all else, we can battle against the trials that come against us. Our role as ezer warriors allows us access to an arsenal of characteristic traits, blessings, and clarity to know when to step up to battle and when to bow before the King who has already won the war. Scripture has a myriad of examples of God's people going to battle only to have it already won. They still had to put on the armor, take up their arms, and march to the battlefield. They still had to prepare and train beforehand. But the victory was always in the hands of the Lord.

Ladies, we are more than a pretty face or a kind word. We are more than our past has tried to dictate and more than any person can presume. We are beloved and chosen to wage war against the enemy. The question is, are you willing?

"WE ARE MORE THAN OUR PAST HAS TRIED TO DICTATE AND MORE THAN ANY PERSON CAN PRESUME. WE ARE BELOVED AND CHOSEN TO WAGE WAR AGAINST THE ENEMY. THE QUESTION IS, ARE YOU WILLING?"

CHAPTER ELEVEN

OUR BATTLE CRY
PHOEBE | ROMANS 16

C an I be honest with you? I think we've established a decent rapport by this point to warrant the trust. Some of my greatest hurts have been from well-intentioned men who belittled me without even realizing that's what they were doing. They would make comments that came across as patronizing. It was the equivalent of the Southern phrase, "Bless your heart." It may be coated and presented as something sweet, but it is still just a dirty mud pie covered in the sweet whipped-cream compliment. It looks like something wonderful, but the reality is a disappointment.

This unfortunately was also true within the church walls. I've shared a couple of stories of my experiences with Godly men who still treated me as someone lacking. They would treat me as if I should be honored that they, these amazing men called by God, would trust me enough to sit in the meeting even though my voice was rarely heard. This wasn't (isn't) always the case. There are plenty of men both inside and outside of the church who recognize the shared authority God has given to both men and women. I have had blessed experiences with men who trust and encourage my calling from God, not questioning me but instead empowering me to fulfill all that God has placed in my heart to do.

There is an article written by Jack Hayford, a trusted and respected voice in the church, that discusses women in ministry. He explains the original relationship between man and woman as mutual rather than simply equal. In the beginning they weren't Adam and Eve, but simply *adam* which means mankind. No name distinguished them for they were one as God is three in one. But then in the fall, God tells the woman that her desire will be for her husband and he will rule over her–the divide of the curse reflecting in all parts, including authority[38]. I believe I've said this throughout, but I want to reiterate: the call of Skull Crushers is not to raise rebellion within the hearts of women, lashing out against the male-dictated dogma that permeates the halls of our churches. Rebellion in any form is not honoring God. He wants a submitted spirit. He wants a malleable spirit. He wants us to let go of our own biased preconceptions and allow Him to guide and direct us. He wants our hearts to be open so that He can speak through us and use us in the ways that are needed. He is the one who elevates us. This isn't about equal opportunity, feminist agendas. This isn't about eliminating the differences between men and women. God designed men and women to be different, but equally beautiful. Equally reflections of our creator. Skull Crushers is about recognizing that women are equally made in the image of God, and He has called us to be His spiritual warriors. As we've seen in the previous women's lives, this can look different for each of us. Some are called to be out front and bold in our proclamations. Others of us are called to a more subdued role that can appear to play into the assumed "proper" roles for women. They are all vital to the kingdom! Every role God calls us to is integral to what He is accomplishing and all point to one thing: Jesus. We don't want secondary issues to detract from the main focus, which is the saving grace of Jesus Christ. We are looking into the lives and

---

[38] Hayford, Jack. *A Woman's Place in Christ.* Jack Hayford Ministries. https://www.jackhayford.org/teaching/articles/a-womans-place-in-christ/. Accessed 2/5/2022

stories of these women, not to stir the pot needlessly, but to see how we as women in the church, mutually called and appointed by God, can step out boldly when we receive that call.

One of the areas I serve in my church is through a group that is called Women's Equip. Our equip classes are similar to what other churches may refer to as their Sunday School classes. They cover a multitude of topics from foundational knowledge for new believers, freedom classes that dig into spiritual warfare and bondage, and even stewardship and finances. We have classes that focus on the Jewish faith and tradition, and we've recently started the Women's Equip classes that speak directly to our women, sharing our church's heart for women and encouraging them in their roles as believers. The first session of this curriculum was all about confidence. We began by discussing why we could be confident in God–in who He is–then progressed to being confident in who we are as women and finished with being confident in our purposes. Because we are confident in who God is, we can trust who He says we are and what He lays on our heart for us to do. If I as a believer and submitted follower of Jesus have the Holy Spirit living in me, I can hear Him speak to me. I can feel Him prompting me and guiding me along my life. We say for our kids that there is no junior Holy Spirit, the same is true for the women of God. There isn't a separate, "lesser" Holy Spirit guiding us, keeping us confined to shadows. If you as a woman of God feel the call of God on your life, trust that calling!

Romans 8:28 says, "We know that all things work together for the good of those who love God, who are called according to His purpose" (CSB). There aren't stipulations in this verse. There isn't a hidden clause or a members-only addition.

In Luke we find the story of Mary and Martha. Many believers have heard this story used to preach against busyness or about the importance of focusing on Jesus rather than allowing life to be a distraction. But we miss the cultural component of this story that would have been so shocking at the time. First, we need to understand the difference in eastern learning versus western learning. In the West, we study by dissecting. We pull things apart and dig into each individual meaning of each word. We exegete to understand. And there is nothing wrong with this. In fact, it's a method that I love and readily use as well. But in the Middle East, the Jewish rabbis wouldn't teach by giving their students a portion of scripture to pull apart and evaluate. They would teach in stories and parables. They would allow scriptures to speak for themselves, rather than pull them apart to speculate the meanings. And while they taught, the students would sit at their feet to absorb the information. They would literally follow their rabbi, emulating what he did so that they, too, could go and do the same thing. It was less information gathering and more of a lifestyle internship. With that in mind, let's read what Luke recorded about the interaction with Mary and Martha:

While they were traveling, he entered a village, and a woman named Martha welcomed him into her home. She had a sister named Mary, who also sat at the Lord's feet and was listening to what he said. But Martha was distracted by her many tasks, and she came up and asked, "Lord, don't you care that my sister has left me to serve alone? So tell her to give me a hand." The Lord answered her, "Martha, Martha, you are worried and upset about many things, but one thing is necessary. Mary has made the right choice, and it will not be taken away from her" (Luke 10:38-42, CSB).

There are several counter-cultural points in this passage but let's just look at Jesus' response to Martha about what Mary was doing. Culture (and many traditional doctrines) would say that Mary shouldn't be at the feet of Jesus. It would recognize that it was a place for the men who were following and learning from Jesus as their rabbi. They would say that she was okay to be in the room, but her role was relegated to helping and serving the men. Jesus instead let Martha know that Mary (and Martha as well) was welcome to learn at His feet. He told her that, in fact, it was the best place to be.

Only in very recent history have women's lives and reputations been their own. Even that is still not inclusive to all countries and cultures. Some cultures still function under traditional roles where the woman's reputation directly reflects upon the man who is responsible for her—be it her husband, father, or other male family member. How they dress, how they act, how they respond to others is all under the umbrella of influence by that senior male. This wasn't (isn't) always about control, but rather protection. When some saw no issue with treating women as less-than, women had to have a male representative to protect their rights and interests.

The assumption has always been that the Israelites were a patriarchal society. This was certainly the case by the first century AD, but what about before then? During what is known as the Intertestamental Period (or Deuterocanonical Period to Catholic and Orthodox Christians), there was a shift in the Jewish faith. This was the period when records say God was silent. Prophets didn't hear Him speak, there was no indication of what was going on or foretelling of what would happen. For 400 years between the Old Testament and the New Testament, the Israelites underwent massive governmental shifts.

It began with the Persians. They technically showed up before the official time frame (they conquered Babylon in 536 BC), but they were the ones in power when this time period began. It was the Persians who allowed the Israelites to return to Jerusalem and had a fairly generous foreign policy, tolerant to the Jewish faith.

After the Persians came Alexander the Great and the Greeks. This is when women began to see a culture of shame shift onto them. The

Greeks not only took over land and territory, but they implemented Hellenization. Hellenization is the adoption of Greek culture and religion. Everywhere they went, they sought to rid that region of its own unique culture and indoctrinate them instead into Greek culture. For the pious Jews, this was an outrage. Greek culture was full of idols and fluid promiscuity. In an effort to counter the attack, Ben Sira theology began to take hold, which caused women to lose much of their social standing. Kristi McLelland describes it as, "...pious, virtuous Jewish men who stood up against the invasion of Hellenism and 'Vegas' took it too far."[39]

From the Greeks to the Egyptians, following the death of Alexander the Great, Jewish worship shifted some more, allowing two main religious mindsets to surface: Pro-Syrian Hellenizing and the Orthodox Jew (which was a predecessor to the Pharisee). From there, the Jews experienced the takeover of the Syrians—who completely defiled their faith—the Maccabean Era—from which the Pharisees and Sadducees emerged—and finally the Roman Empire took over around 63 BC.

All of the turmoil they experienced caused the women to lose their place of honor and instead be relegated to a place of shame. When Jesus came, He turned the tables for women and re-established that place of honor. Women had a place at His table, and He welcomed them in His ministry. The woman at the well was the first person to whom He revealed Himself as the Messiah, the women at His tomb were the first to know of His resurrection, and He laid the foundation for women to continue to play integral roles within the ministry of the early church. Including Phoebe, a deacon in the church.

Ladies, we are not relegated to a single area of service. Our callings and purposes aren't limited to what culture has decided over the

---

[39] McLelland, Kristi. *Jesus and Women in the First Century.* Session Two. Lifeway. 2019 Nashville. Page 33

years. Our only focus should be on hearing and absorbing the words of our Lord and Savior. Rather than trying to fit into a predetermined role or expending needless energy fighting against that designation, we should look to what Jesus says is the right choice. We should be so attuned with the voice of Jesus that there is no question when we hear Him speak our purposes over us. It won't matter if culture agrees, or certain people within the church, or our neighbors, or our own family. What matters is that when we hear the word of Jesus speak, our hearts believe it and obey its direction. He won't contradict His own word so if there is any question at all, look to scriptures (in context!). It's okay to have several trusted mentors or advisors that speak into your life and pray over you, but trust in the word of God over any word of man. Remember that "no one can derail you from your destiny except you."[40]

We Are Mutually Called.

One of the women who played a vital role in the early church was Phoebe. We're introduced to her through a passing mention in Romans: "I commend to you our sister Phoebe, a deacon of the church in Cenchreae" (Romans 16:1, NIV). To commend someone is to recommend and formally introduce. This would be Paul's way of telling the Roman church, "Here is the person I have sent to assist you and teach you in my place." He is making it clear that he trusts her implicitly.

Phoebe was a deacon. There are commentaries that like to insist that the word used in Romans 16:1 referring to Phoebe as diakonos *might* also mean deacon, but in this case it *must* only mean servant or helper. Simply put, they are wrong. Phoebe was a deacon. There is really no reason to belabor this point as there is now a large majority that agree with this simple statement. So why is it important?

---

[40] Morris, Robert. 2019, *Why Am I Here? Study Guide.* Gateway Publishing.

It's important because we need to recognize what being a deacon actually means. First Timothy 3 gives us the qualifications for deacons.

The same goes for those who want to be servants in the church: serious, not deceitful, not too free with the bottle, not in it for what they can get out of it. They must be reverent before the mystery of the faith, not using their position to try to run things. Let them prove themselves first. If they show they can do it, take them on. No exceptions are to be made for women—same qualifications: serious, dependable, not sharp-tongued, not overfond of wine. Servants in the church are to be committed to their spouses, attentive to their own children, and diligent in looking after their own affairs. Those who do this servant work will come to be highly respected, a real credit to this Jesus-faith (1 Timothy 3:8-13, MSG).

I listed The Message version because it does a fantastic job of clarifying that this wasn't a position only available to men. The qualifications for female deacons were to be the same standard as men. But what we miss is–like in the story about Mary learning at the feet of Jesus–how countercultural this was. The early church dealt with more challenges than simply sharing the amazing Gospel of Jesus. They fought against the same struggles that God warned the Israelites about when they entered the Promised Land.

The reason God was so intentional about eradicating false gods was because He knew the fallacy of the heart of Man. The fall of Israel ultimately came because of this. Even Solomon built altars for the gods and idols of his many wives. In doing so he allowed atrocious practices to enter into the kingdom and it ultimately pulled his heart away from God.

Like I mentioned earlier about the history of how Hellenization affected the rights of women, the early church was still heavily influenced by Greek philosophers and their false ideals about religion and women. Paul's letters were to clarify the difference of Christianity and emphasize the heart of God. Philosophy said that women were a distraction and evil–this led to the medieval misunderstanding that even marriage was a distraction for those called to serve God. Paul emphasized that men were to love and care for their wives as intently as Jesus loved the church. Greek culture restricted women's rights to being little more than prisoners within their own homes, not allowed an education and certainly not welcome to join in discussion about "higher ideals." In direct contrast, the early church allowed and encouraged women to join in worship and hear God for themselves. Challenges arose when people compared the church to other religions that readily practiced orgies and prostitution as part of their worship. His goal was never to marginalize women but empower them within the church. By acknowledging the role that Phoebe had, he continued to elevate and encourage female leaders within the church.

I don't think there are many who would try to claim that women don't hear the voice of God. They may insist that women hear differently (perhaps insinuating that it's somehow less-than), but if you talk to any believer longer than a couple of minutes it becomes abundantly clear that we all hear God differently. How He speaks to me is not going to be the same as how he speaks to you–and for that I am so grateful! We serve a God who is infinitely multi-faceted and who has the ability to have a unique relationship with each of His children.

When I was younger, I heard God speak in reassurances. He would provide opportunities for me to know Him and His great love for me. In all my years, including (especially) those that included my seasons of rebellion, I knew God loved me. It is the one fact about God that I have never once questioned. I know this is not true for others. But as I grew and as I began to understand more about who

God created me to be, I began to experience other pieces of God's character. In the last decade, I have been in a season of growth in the Spirit–learning who the Holy Spirit is, how He works in my life, what it feels like to be filled with Him so that I recognize when I stray away from Him. It has allowed me to better appreciate how individual God is to each of His children and why there are so many names for God throughout scripture.

When God first called me to write and speak, I had been a Christian for about a decade and a half. I thought I knew God well. I knew I heard Him speak to me. I knew the basics of what it meant to live out my faith in my everyday life. I led Bible studies, had worked in both a Christian nonprofit and a church, and was a leader within the church we attended. In my strategic-based mind, it made sense. But it was less of a calling and more of an invitation. When I accepted that calling–which looked like nothing more than telling God yes during my prayer time–what I didn't realize was that was also my accepting God's invitation to go deeper with Him. He used that moment to launch me into the season of getting to know Him more. It was in those early days that I first felt a shift in my spirit about moving. I am a 6th generation Floridian and all of my family lives there. It was comfortable and I had no real inclination to move anywhere else. I can't really describe it beyond a shift in my spirit. One day I had no desire to live anywhere else, and the next day, when the idea of moving came to mind I was okay with it. I believe that, too, was an invitation from God–wanting to know if I really would follow where He was leading.

Not long after that I experienced my first vision. During a time of worship, while my eyes were closed, I had a mental picture appear. I didn't recognize the shape, but it appeared like a piece of a map with one specific location glowing radiant and bright. Unsure what to do with it, I went home and drew it on our bathroom mirror, noting the glowing point with a star. My husband came in, looked at it, and without any further thought or context informed me that it looked like Fort Worth, Texas. I turned to look at him and said with confidence I didn't know I had, "Well, I think we're supposed to move there."

While my husband grew up in Austin, Texas, and we had friends who lived in Dallas, Texas, we knew next to nothing about Fort Worth. My husband, who had been wanting to move someplace else but was in a personal time of surrendering that particular desire to God, took it as the gift and direction it was. He began looking for opportunities to transfer within his company. In less than six months, he had a job offer (coordinating with a promotion) that would transfer us to Fort Worth, Texas. That was in January of 2014.

Since then, my husband jokes with me that I've gone full-blown charismatic. Not meaning any insult to those who are, simply that my walk with the Holy Spirit went from the shallows to the deep end. We laugh because I grew up in a church that loved God but certainly never walked out in the gifts of the Spirit. Each new church I became a part of was a step further from the safety of religion and deeper into the unknown of a dynamic relationship with a God so far beyond my understanding that it will take an eternity to know Him. I received a prayer language that enhanced my quiet time and caused me to begin to press in more when I intercede for others. I began to function in the prophetic, receiving words in due season for my own life as well as for others around me. It wasn't weird, out of control, mysticism. It was learning new facets of the character of the same God I had always known. It was just the next step of the journey God was (is) taking me on.

As that journey continued, it allowed more opportunity for me to speak and teach. When it comes to teaching, traditionally, women are inevitably relegated to the world of children and women's ministry. There is nothing wrong with that if that's where God is calling you! I love speaking to women's groups. Obviously, I can more readily relate and (clearly) God has certainly called me to write for women wanting to grow in their walk with God. It wasn't that I didn't want to teach in those areas, it was that I didn't want to be limited by someone's directive that those were the only options available to me and other women who are called to reach the masses.

In the Old Testament, we find incredible, Godly, female leaders. Deborah is an obvious example as one of the judges of Israel. The judges in those days were less like the legal judge just sitting behind a bench, only listening to the concerns of the people, and more like a general in the military, making decisions about war and readily engaging in battles. Barak wouldn't go to battle unless Deborah came with him. He wanted her leadership and her anointing on it. In the New Testament, women were leaders among the early church. When scripture refers to the meeting in their homes, that was often synonymous with pastoring that meeting. The main verses used to silence women in the church are often used as standalones, rather than within context.

In the case of 1 Timothy 2, where Paul says that women are to remain silent, the word silent is *hesuchia*. Rather than the understanding of not speaking at all, it would be better perceived as having a quiet spirit. This idea of stillness is not relegated to women (though this verb is feminine), as we should all long for peace and a contented spirit. It's also important to note that these verses are written to wives, not all women. It is addressing specifics within marriage and how we relate to our husbands. I mentioned in the first chapter that while the verses for women are often taken out of context to stifle, if we continue reading through the directive to the husbands, we find that where wives are called to submit (respect) their husbands, husbands are in turn called to "love their wives as Christ loves the church," i.e. sacrificially. If that isn't an even greater call of submission, I don't know what is. The marriage relationship is one of equal love and respect. Submission is not about subjugation. It isn't giving anyone the power to dictate our every word or decision. The mutual submission that we're called to in marriage relationships is about putting someone else's best interest ahead of your own. It's not about control and who's in charge.

My husband knew that I was strong-willed before we began dating. Once we were in a relationship, he didn't expect me to suddenly wilt and allow him to walk all over me. He appreciates my opinion and I often irritate him more if I act the submissive victim rather than the strong-willed, opinionated woman he married. In fact, during one of our arguments, I was busy blubbering and apologizing and he fussed at me, "What are you apologizing for? You didn't do anything wrong!" There is a difference between being submitted with a quiet and peaceful spirit and being silent.

Women, stop apologizing for speaking the word that God has given you. Stop justifying the ministry God has called you to start and lead. Stop blubbering about how you know men are supposed to be the leader and all, but you want to be a part. Just stop. Stop using misinterpretations to disqualify yourself. If God has placed the desire to lead or teach or speak or care or do whatever, then doing anything besides that is disobedience.

Another common verse used to disqualify women in ministry is found in 1 Corinthians. If we go back to the beginning of the letter, 1 Corinthians 1:11 addresses the reason for his letter, saying, "For it has been reported to me about you, my brothers and sisters, by members of Chloe's people, that there is rivalry among you" (CSB). Another version specifically says, "Chloe's house church." Chloe– a woman–was the leader of the church that met in her home. A more direct way of saying this is that Chloe was one of the pastors. Knowing that, why would Paul then proceed to tell the church–who had good female leadership–that women weren't allowed to speak?

It isn't about muzzling women, rather addressing a specific concern to recognize that there are appropriate times to speak out and times to remain quiet and listen. It's more about addressing a specific instance, with a specific woman, who needed to learn self-control. It goes back to that quiet spirit and keeping the peace.

There are times that I have a lot of opinions and I want to tell people. I want them to know what I have to say and for them to agree with me. I have learned, however, that there is a time and a place to speak out against certain situations–and that time is sometimes never. I have come to terms that while my opinion may be correct, it's not always appropriate to supersede others in authority. It's not my place.

Men and women are mutually called. John 10:10 says, "I have come so that they may have life and have it in abundance" (CSB). Ephesians 3:20-21 says, "Now to Him who is able to do exceedingly abundantly above all that we ask or think, according to the power that works in us, to Him *be* glory in the church by Christ Jesus to all generations, forever and ever" (NKJV). Now tell me how the same God who came to give us abundant life, the same God who is able to do above and beyond what we can even imagine, would put stifling limitations on half of His creation? Why would God, who has blessed *all* of us with "every spiritual blessing" (Ephesians 1:3) put a limitation on what He can do with us simply based on our sex?

He has given us each a unique voice and desires for us to work together to build His Kingdom. God also loves order, not chaos. There are plenty of studies that more than prove women have more words to say than men. Stereotypes exist because there is a thread of truth to them. Women being more talkative is one of them. Even though I am not a particularly talkative person and often don't relate with this, I understand it. I see it in my marriage when I come to a decision and opinion long before my husband who takes time to sort through the options and possibilities. I see it in the workplace when I see an issue and want to just go and handle it while my male co-workers are more apt to evaluate it and be slower in their response. I believe this is an intentional design by a loving Father who wanted His kids to collaborate. I believe that it is a balance and opportunity for us as brothers and sisters in Christ to recognize the strengths of each other and realize there are times and places for both responses. Our differences allow us to understand the multi-faceted nature of a God who is neither male nor female. It allows us to relate to God as our Father and also as a mother (Isaiah 49:15 and Isaiah 66:13).

Paul wasn't seeking to silence women from preaching or teaching. He wasn't saying that women couldn't be leaders in the church or ministry. He was recognizing issues that develop from us not acknowledging and appreciating the differences between men and women, knowing we each have something vitally important to bring to the table. If men were in charge of bringing the main dish, spiritual meat if you will, but didn't even consider the need for a serving tray and utensils, we would find it incredibly difficult to enjoy and partake in that meal. It's not about who is in control–we're all necessary to offer the world a complete image of who God is.

We Are Servants.

While there is limited detail about Phoebe in scripture, what we can clearly see is that she was servant hearted. Being a deacon requires that. Submitting to one another is not a thing of lessening our calling or worth. Nowhere in the Bible does it say that women should submit to men. It does, however, call us to respect everyone. We should be submitting to both men and women, honoring one another as we would honor Christ. We're told as wives to submit to our husbands because marriage is the example of Christ and the church. The church is to submit to Christ, honoring Him and respecting Him.

Likewise, as we just said, husbands are called to love their wives as Christ loved the church. That is sacrificial. None of these relationships are meant to be domineering or demanding. Jesus lowered himself to become man. Then just before dying on a cross for all of us, he furthered the example and washed the feet of his disciples. Some may point to the wives about submission, but Christ submitted himself to His disciples and husbands are called to love their wives that same way. It's equal submission. It's mutual leadership.

Women are traditionally better at empathy than men. The whole maternal instinct if you will. Whether that's the case or it's simply a matter of closer observation and willingness to address feelings, this allows us a unique perspective on humanity as whole.

I have a friend and pastor who has taught in depth on how Jesus washing the disciples' feet reflects this humbling picture of us in our humanity. So often we look at it and think sure, okay, that's a little gross, but we remove ourselves from the details of the time and imagine the modern-day foot washing ceremonies instead. Now, these are beautiful reminders, especially when incorporated into a marriage ceremony, taking the time to show the other person that we're willing to submit before them and care for them. But we're missing the nasty, putrefied humanity of what Jesus was demonstrating. The roads in Jesus' day were not sanitary. They weren't neatly paved and kept free of litter. They were dirt, covered in the fecal matter of the animals that also shared the space. Even with sandals, their feet would have been covered in remnants of their journey there. Covered in that which they walked through. And Jesus knelt before them and intimately cleaned their feet, a job typically relegated to the lowest servant of the home. He cleansed the dirt, grime, and literal poop off of their feet, making them clean before Him—by His actions. We too have been cleaned of the remnants of our journey and made pure by the actions of Jesus. We too have been called to clean the feet of others. We're called to kneel before others, giving them a safe place to come no matter where they have journeyed from nor what they have journeyed through. It's in that safety that they can encounter the healing cleansing of Jesus for themselves. It's in that place of humility and servitude that we can create spaces for us as humans to come together, acknowledge our humanity and the mess we've made of it, and then allow the Holy Spirit to do the work of making us pure and holy.

Being servant-minded is not the same as the idea of a lower-class. It's losing sight of the need for recognition and applause and simply doing the work placed before you. There is a young man who works at our church who has the true heart of a servant. I first met him as one of the kid's ministry workers on the weekends. Then he expanded that role to also be an intern for our student ministry. Currently, he is on staff as a member of our facilities team. Meanwhile, he still serves in both student and kids' ministries.

I asked him what he thought about his job one time, and he responded, "It's not that I particularly like cleaning or anything, but I can do it well and it's teaching me attention to detail. It also gives me a lot of quiet time with God, so He's been downloading a lot during this time." Another staff member joked that he was now equipped to be the perfect husband–able to clean and handle children with ease.

Joking aside, I loved his perspective. He said he feels called to vocational ministry, but this is where he needs to be in this season. He serves with grace and a smile, no matter if it's teaching the 6th graders an awesome, engaging lesson from the platform or whether it's emptying the trash cans after an event.

We're all called to serve others. It might not look like sanitizing a kid's playscape (though let's talk about how awesome those individuals who brave that truly are!). But it might look like picking up the coffee cups left after the small group meeting. It might look like making copies for one of your ministries. It might look like doing the lunch run during crunch time at work. It might look like holding the door and smiling at a mom who is dragging a screaming child out of the store, looking embarrassed and unsure of her calling as a mother. We don't need to complicate it. We just need to do it.

Provide the safe space for people to be human (we all are, afterall). Humble yourself and your heart. Then simply serve in the space before you.

My vocational job right now is as a coordinator in our adult ministry, specifically working with the small groups. I help people find a small group to join and help others start up and manage their own small group. I can honestly say that small groups are one of the easiest and most effective ways to serve others. And I'm not just saying that because it's my job. It's so much more than just a Bible study.

The group I am currently a member of has developed into our extended family. We were new to the neighborhood when a woman and her teenage daughter walked by our house. They had accidentally received someone else's mail and were hand delivering it to the correct house. Being that they hadn't met us before and wanted to meet all their neighbors, they introduced themselves to us. In this brief, five-minute interaction, they invited us to their small group that was just starting up.

My husband and I had been trying to find a small group we could both attend since we first moved to the area and up to that point had not found the right fit. Whether due to schedules or personality or whatever, we just hadn't been able to build any real connections with a lot of couples. But we were willing to try, and this family was willing to step out to extend the invitation.

174

Two years later, they are some of our closest friends. We still have scheduling conflicts that occasionally prevent us from attending, but we have established a lasting relationship. We do life together and can serve one another. When my husband was out of the country over my birthday, they cooked me a special dinner and took the time to celebrate with me. When the world shut down due to COVID-19, we would set up what we called porch hangouts. I brought one of my camping chairs down to their house, set up on the sidewalk while she sat in her chair on her porch. We maintained the required distance for the time but were able to meet a legitimate need of social interaction when we were all so sequestered. We celebrate together, we pray over each other, we support each other through painful seasons, we serve and love each other.

Being servant-minded doesn't have to be overly complicated. Holding a door, picking up the trash when you see it even if it's not yours, babysitting for a mom friend who needs a nap, taking a meal to someone who was sick, praying for others. There are so many possibilities! Even with something like hosting a small group, we don't need to overcomplicate it. Find any space–whether at your home or the local coffee shop–set a time and be available. That's really all it is.

Leadership isn't relegated to only a select few. Any and all of us are able and capable because we have a mighty Benefactor who has led by example and calls us to likewise step out and be benefactors for others.

WE ARE BENEFACTORS.

Romans 16:2 says, "So you should welcome her in the Lord in a manner worthy of the saints and assist her in whatever matter she may require your help. **For indeed she has been a benefactor of**

many — and of me also" (CSB, emphasis mine). When I was studying Phoebe initially, I got caught up on the word "benefactor." And like other times when I got stuck on something, I trudged through and found a way to make it work. What I wrote unintentionally boxed in this particular asset as comparable to a cheerleader—knowing that we are called to support and champion the things in our lives–but being a benefactor is so much more than cheering from the sidelines while others do the work.

Phoebe was not just a passing churchgoer of no consequence, and she did more than just cheer on her fellow male leaders. Not only was she a deacon in the early church, but she was also believed to have been responsible for delivering Paul's letter to the Roman church, a role that included offering clarification on anything written in the letter and generally offering wisdom and teaching as needed. That is included in what Romans 16:2 refers to when it tells us, "For she has been a benefactor of many–and of me also" (CSB). I want to look at this mention of Phoebe two separate ways. The first will be the surface value of a benefactor in the commonly understood sense, and the second will dig into the wording a little, because we know that Paul was very intentional in the words he chose to use in his letters. Both evaluations make it clear that she was a vital member of Paul's team. She was able to offer her leadership and wisdom to the work that Paul was accomplishing and actively helping impact the kingdom.

Here's the simple truth: we can all help the cause by leading from wherever we are. Seasons change and so those things that we are surrounded by will change as well. Right now, I am a mom to three kids, two in elementary school and one just starting middle school. I have one daughter who is into dance and theater, one who is an avid soccer player, and one who isn't sure what he wants to do but is obsessed with video games, the human body, and generally just driving his sisters crazy. I try my best to be my kids' biggest–and loudest–cheerleader. My middle daughter can attest to that at her soccer games. I come by this naturally as my mom regularly lost her voice during my band and lacrosse seasons. But championing my kids doesn't just involve getting them to all their activities. It looks like running lines for an audition with my oldest daughter. It looks like taking my middle daughter for a run to help her condition for soccer or doing a puzzle with her to foster her love of problem solving. It looks like finding new activities for my son to try out as he decides what he is passionate about doing. It looks like reading God's word with my kids so we can have discussions about it, and I can train them up in the way they should go so they will develop a personal relationship with God for themselves (Proverbs 22:6).

I am also a wife to an engineer. There isn't much I can vocally cheer for, but I can go to work events with him, be a sounding board for him when needed, and encourage him in the things that bring him joy–like working out, writing parody songs, and serving in our 4th through 6th grade ministry at church.

We naturally promote and champion things that are near and dear to us. We throw our support behind those things whether in the money we spend, the time we invest, or the voice we lend. My family is my top priority behind my relationship with God, so they get my biggest support, but there are other areas I'm able to lend support to as well. The definition of a benefactor is someone or something that provides help or an advantage of some sort. Being a benefactor to the Kingdom of God means that we play a part in helping advance the kingdom.

I've said before that I believe that Satan is less concerned about whether or not we're saved and more concerned with making us ineffective. We're the biggest hindrance to others experiencing the wonder and might of a personal relationship with God. Despite knowing this outcome, God still chose to partner with us.

Being a benefactor also means that we might serve in a less visible role. The lack of spotlight does not diminish the vitalness or authority of a role. Deacons are vital members of the church leadership, but unless it's communion or helping at the altar during prayer, you don't really see them. Their role is supporting the ministry wherever it needs.

My daughter's love for theater has led us to finding classes to help foster her in growing in this area. Most recently we signed her up for a combo class that will cover acting, singing, and dancing. They have the classes separated out by ages, starting as young as six years old and continuing through to classes for adults. One of the adult classes is called "The Real MVPs: Props, Costumes, and Stage Management." For a play to be successful, it must be more than simply the actors saying their lines. You need these "real MVPs." You need the tech team to help balance the music and mics. You need a team to determine the lighting. You need a team of people to help backstage and get everyone on their marks at just the right time. There are so many roles beyond just those you see. The same is true in ministry.

Benefactors aren't necessarily the ones on the platform or in front of a crowd, but they are incredibly vital. Whether by finances, support, advice, or other services, Phoebe was able to play a vital role in the early church, not only to Paul but, as he said, to many others as well. It was part of who she was, and it is a part of who we are called to be as ezers.

Like I said earlier, we're going to look at this verse a little more in depth. We've seen that often benefactors are a type of unsung hero. But when we look closer to the word Paul used for benefactor, we discover there is something so incredible hidden in the phrasing of this. If you do a word search on this verse and look at the cross referencing, the word used for benefactor is *prostatis*. *Prostatis* is the Greek word that can mean patroness, or benefactor, but another way to define this is "helper." More specifically, "a woman set over others; a female guardian, a protectress." Do you see it? Paul was recognizing that Phoebe was an ezer! It alludes to phrasing that was used when Genesis tells us, "Then the LORD God said, 'It is not good for the man to be alone. I will make **a helper** corresponding to him'" (Genesis 2:18, CSB).

Our roles are going to look different for each of us and in each season. There might be a time when you play a supporting role. There might also be a time when you play a very visible role. No matter what, it doesn't affect who we are, simply how God is choosing to partner with us at that time. Whether you are a behind-the-scenes benefactor, serving after hours, or standing on the stage teaching in front of thousands, know that God has chosen you. He wants His daughters to be active participants in what He is doing in and through the church. The title of that role does not change the fact that we are all created as ezers. He has equipped us to be victorious in this spiritual war, the only question is are you willing to say yes when He calls your name?

"WE SHOULD BE SO ATTUNED WITH THE VOICE OF JESUS THAT THERE IS NO QUESTION WHEN WE HEAR HIM SPEAK OUR PURPOSES OVER US."

CHAPTER TWELVE
THE WARRIOR
INSIDE US ALL
INSERT YOUR NAME HERE |
ETERNITY

This chapter isn't an afterthought even though it is the last in the book. It's an intentional reminder that each of the women we've looked at from the Bible were just regular women, living their lives, and serving God as He called them. I know when I read these stories or passages, it's easy to distance myself. It's easy to read it from the outside looking in, but not really connecting or relating to what's written. But we're an extension of this same story.

From the dawn of creation to the establishment of New Jerusalem, God is actively writing His love story and we get to be actively involved. While we might not have put on physical armor (though some of you might), we do need to put on spiritual armor because we have been conscripted to fight in the ultimate battle of life and death. The good news is we already know who wins.

As I researched–reading through the scripture in various versions, commentaries of those specific verses, books on overall subject matters, and articles of history and interpretation–there were times that I had to walk away. I would read ideas that people fully believed that would pull at my gut, leaving me irate and discouraged. I would talk with people who had similar viewpoints and people who had completely different viewpoints. I tried to set aside my personal opinions and approach this with an open mind and heart, wanting God to be the one who ultimately revealed the truth to me.

We all come from a place of bias, but we're also created with brains that can be rewired. Just because we were told something our entire lives doesn't make it inherently true. That's not to say that we all need to discard everything that was taught to us in our youth–some of you have been raised to recognize God's truth and walk in that way. But it is important to remain grace-filled. You see, there was a consistent vein that served as a trigger each time I would begin to feel my stomach clench and anxiety rise. It can be summarized in a quote from a man who was considered a defender of the Christian faith during his life in the first century: "Woman...do you not know that you are (each) an Eve? The sentence of God on this sex of yours lives in this age: the guilt must of necessity live too. You are the devil's gateway...."[41]

What does that quote do inside of you? Some of you may feel mad, others may feel hurt. Maybe you feel disgusted that this came from someone who is recognized as being a defender of the faith. Whatever you feel, I have a word of encouragement for you: this is not God's heart for women. No matter how someone interprets the Bible, one thing I can promise you is that God never shames us. Jesus came to remove shame, so how could His promises then be

---

[41] John Temple Bristow. *What Paul Really Said About Women.* pp. 28 Harper & Row, New York, NY. 1988

twisted to point the finger of shame back on someone? This is the crux of the matter. If you are reading something and you feel shame, that is not of God. Jesus came to bring us into right standing with God, not point the finger of blame. John said in one of his letters, "If we confess our sins, he is faithful and righteous to forgive us our sins and to cleanse us from all unrighteousness" (1 John 1:9, CSB). That promise isn't circumstantial beyond simply accepting what is being offered. Jesus makes this same offer to each and every person, fulfilling the need for both justice and mercy. There isn't a separate clause for women because we are supposedly the "devil's gateway" to bring destruction down upon the heads of God's holy creation of man. We're all broken. We've all messed up. Man or woman, the Bible confirms that all of us have fallen short of the glory of God (Romans 3:23). In fact, it's in that same letter to the church of Rome that Paul reminds us that it is God who justifies. "Who can bring an accusation against God's elect? God is the one who justifies" (Romans 8:33, CSB). This idea of pointing the finger of accusation is nothing more than an idea from the pits of hell to alienate God's beloved daughters and limit the impact that they could have on the Kingdom and the work of the Church.

Hebrews tells us "And every priest stands daily at his service, offering repeatedly the same sacrifices, which can never take away sins. But when Christ had offered for all time a single sacrifice for sins, he sat down at the right hand of God, waiting from that time until his enemies should be made a footstool for his feet. For by a single offering, he has perfected for all time those who are being sanctified" (Hebrews 10:11-14, CSB). We don't have to do the work because Jesus has already done it. I love these verses because it reminds me that we don't have to strive for that which Jesus already did.

My senior year of high school I made a vital discovery that has since helped me in my studies: I don't like busy work. That may seem like an obvious observation–not many people actually like busy work, but it was the first time that I was able to recognize my learning style and offered an explanation as to why I struggled in a standard classroom. It wasn't the work itself–I was smart enough to do most of the assignments given to me throughout the years, but when teachers gave assignments that weren't related to the materials or were just time-fillers to meet the required seat-time for each period, I checked out. However, my senior year of high school I switched to a full-time, dual-enrollment at the local community college. I went to class, took notes during the lecture, and then was able to leave. There wasn't a required seat-time to meet government standards. There wasn't filler if a professor couldn't make it to the lecture–it was just canceled. I still learned a great deal but didn't feel like time was just being wasted.

The verses in Hebrews remind us that while the priests of old had to continually offer sacrifices for the sins of the people, Jesus' sacrifice fulfilled the requirement of justice to redeem everyone. We don't have to fill the time. We don't have to feel guilty for someone else's mistakes. We don't have to carry the burden of every woman before us who was weighed down with false accusations and guilt. We simply have to accept what is being offered, knowing that God is love and that perfect love does not condemn us for the sins that we've already been forgiven for.

BEGINNING

Allowing God to rewire our understanding is going to be vital for us to move forward. This isn't a new idea, but it is one that is continually questioned. Too many times well-intentioned people will utilize the consequence given to Adam and Eve in Genesis 3 as the accepted and approved standard. Genesis 3 tells us that after they ate the fruit God explained the consequences to their choice.

He said to the woman: I will intensify your labor pains; you will bear children with painful effort. Your desire will be for your husband, yet he will rule over you.

And he said to the man, "Because you listened to your wife and ate from the tree about which I commanded you, 'Do not eat from it': The ground is cursed because of you. You will eat from it by means of painful labor all the days of your life. It will produce thorns and thistles for you, and you will eat the plants of the field. You will eat bread by the sweat of your brow until you return to the ground, since you were taken from it. For you are dust, and you will return to dust" (Genesis 3:16-19, CSB).

This was to be the consequences for their sin–not the new precedent for God's desire on how His creation interacted with each other. The fall led to disunity. In the beginning, man and woman functioned in perfect unity–supporting one another, serving one another, working together, and doing it all alongside God. So I have to wonder why we lean too much into the consequences of sin to set our standard in the church rather than to the original design God created. John Bristow wrote about some interpretations of these consequences in his book, What Paul Really Said About Women, specifically that, "It is characteristic of marriage outside of God's grace. To prescribe that kind of relationship is to advocate living under the penalty of sin imposed upon Adam and Eve, as if Christ brought nothing new to marriage relationships."[42]

Even though Bristow referred directly to marriage, it can be said the same for any interactions between men and women. When we insist on pointing to a single verse saying that the husband will rule over

---

[42] ibid. pp. 18

the wife without accepting the full context of that statement, we miss an opportunity to experience the fullness of God's grace.

In the beginning, God created man and woman in His image. He created Adam first, but Eve was created as his ezer–his equal in every way. She was created as a warrior to help and support Adam in fulfilling the direction God gave them when He blessed them. She was created to be his partner. She was never an afterthought nor intended to be subservient.

Ladies, you are not an afterthought or a mistake. God chose you before the dawn of creation (Ephesians 1) because he wanted you– you beautiful, precious, beloved daughter. He knew what He was doing when He made you female and knew the role you would play. He has great plans for you and has designed you with intention and purpose.

We're too often caught in the trap of our pasts. We believe the lies that we're unqualified because of what we've done or where we've come from. But while the beginning of the story sets up the plot, it doesn't determine the ending. While I'm thankful my beginning was safe and well-loved, I know for many of you that was not the case. You might have been ignored or abused. Perhaps you even experienced a parent or guardian–the person who is supposed to look out for you–telling you that you were worthless and unwanted. But God has always wanted you. He has always loved you. Ephesians 1:5 tells us that "He predestined us to be adopted as sons (and daughters) for himself, according to the good pleasure of His will." The Message version phrases it this way:

Long before he laid down earth's foundations, he had us in mind, had settled on us as the focus of his love, to be made whole and holy by his love. Long, long ago he decided to adopt us into his family through Jesus Christ. (What pleasure he took in planning this!) He wanted us to enter into the celebration of his lavish gift-giving by the hand of his beloved Son.

When we look at our own stories and journeys, we need to know that that moment wasn't really the beginning. Yes, it was the moment when our character was first introduced, but the story we've been born into has been going on for so much longer than any of our lives. We are a vital and necessary piece of the story, but we are not the beginning.

Plotting a story is always interesting to me. Because I rarely write fiction, I don't do it often, but I love reading fiction. I love to discover the arc that the author took to build their world and their character development. I especially love when there is an unexpected turn of events that throws the story arc into a completely different trajectory than it began. That's what Jesus does for our lives.

No matter where the story began, we each face trials along the way. This too is part of scripture. "We know that affliction produces endurance, endurance produces proven character, and proven character produces hope. This hope will not disappoint us, because God's love has been poured out in our hearts through the Holy Spirit who was given to us" (Romans 5:3-5, CSB). Our trials will look different, but that doesn't make them any less trying.

I mentioned that my beginning was safe and filled with love. But as I grew up, I began to see that wasn't always going to be the case. By the time I was in middle school, while my family life was still safe, I found myself on the receiving end of bullies at school. What began as simply making fun of me turned into veiled threats. This led to my feeling the need to be on guard against anyone and everyone, which continued through high school as well. To protect myself, I became overly confident and often abrasive.

This response to people often alienated me, but it also left a hole inside me that I wanted to feel loved. Without realizing it, like I mentioned in an earlier chapter, I became addicted to the idea of love. Not the healthy love from my heavenly Father or the stable love and support that I had from my family. I wanted to feel wanted and my solution was to find that through dating. Unfortunately, this meant that the relationships I was in weren't particularly healthy. I was clingy and dependent, too willing to go along with whatever might make them continue to want to be with me.

It wasn't until I met my husband that he saw this and helped me identify it. Once I was able to call it out, I was able to submit it to God to help me. That doesn't mean I was healed overnight or that there wasn't other lasting damage that was still being processed. It meant that I was able to move past some of the trials in my beginning and see how God was still able to use them to help me grow. I was immediately freed from the oppression but had to daily submit to renewing my mind. The pain that I felt from others allowed my character to build and become more aware of the effect that words have on people. I was able to see how not getting what you think you want can be a tremendous act of mercy and a blessing in the long run. I wouldn't be who I am today had I ended up with any of the boys I previously dated, two of whom I did fall in love with and one of whom I was even engaged to for a time.

I am not who I was and for that I am grateful. Our beginning does not determine our destination, merely the start of how we are getting there. We can look back to the beginning of creation to understand God's heart and desire for His creation, but that isn't the whole story. God used the trial and choices of Adam and Eve to set up the story for what was to come. His desire is for us to remain in perfect union with Him, but He will never force us–that's not love. But He will foresee the need of a savior and set everything in motion to create a way to bring us back to that place.

MIDDLE

The middle of the story is traditionally where the most conflict resides. It's building up to that final point before the place of resolution and conclusion. As we look at the characteristics of who God made us to be and define the tools and skills that He has equipped us with, the more ready we will be to take on those conflicts. What does that mean for us today?

That means that we are going to war. Ladies, I hope you have seen the power and strength that existed in the women from scripture. I hope you have felt a stirring in your own spirit to get out and do something, no longer satisfied to sit back and let other people do it for you.

The church is faltering, not because God is insufficient, but because we have crippled ourselves by sidelining half of our players. We are attacking each other rather than lifting one another up. We are alienating those who are hurting because we can't seem to get beyond our own ideals that don't inherently line up with God's Word. But the church is the bride of Christ and we can do something to change the current trajectory.

Let's look at what we've already gone over in the previous chapters. Through the ten women we've learned from, God has shown us that we are equal, precious vessels, warriors, and encouragers. He's shown us that we are seen, more than any one title, called, equipped, and honored. We are servants. We are benefactors. Ultimately, above anything, we are His beloved daughters.

God has used these ten women to show us that we have influence and authority. They have shown us that each and every one of us is called to be bold, give generously, and declare the truth of who God is. We are called to crush comfort zones, approach with both humility and knowledge, have faith, show initiative, secure blessings, and claim territory. We are called to name with confidence. We are called to change the rules. And we are called to seek God above everything else.

We may only have a single role in the story, but it's a vital role. No one else can play our role and no one else can do what God has placed in our hearts to do for Him. Who we are, what we have been given, and what we are called to do might carry the same names, but how we go about doing it will be as unique and beautiful as each and every one of us.

The enemy wants you sidelined. He wants you to be apathetic and uninterested. He wants you to believe the worst about yourself and about your fellow sisters. The enemy is scared of you because he knows that God has given us full authority over the things that come against us. God has given us the power to take action and make tremendous headway for the Kingdom of God. You are more powerful that you realize! It's not through our strength but by the power of the omnipotent Lord of all creation. The King has called your name and is trusting you to step up to fight in the battles before you. Take back what the enemy has stolen from you. Step forward into the promises of God. Our steps forward crush the enemy's skull as we step into those promises accomplished on the cross. As we step out into our callings. As we step out into our passions. As we step out into who we are meant to be.

END

God has equipped us in who we are, given us implements to wage war, and taught us the techniques that will bring us into the victory He has already secured.

The book of Revelation tells us that there is only one who is worthy–Jesus.

Then I saw in the right hand of the one seated on the throne a scroll with writing on both sides, sealed with seven seals. I also saw a mighty angel proclaiming with a loud voice, "Who is worthy to open the scroll and break its seals?" But no one in heaven or on earth or under the earth was able to open the scroll or even to look in it. I wept and wept because no one was found worthy to open the scroll or even to look in it. Then one of the elders said to me, "Do not weep. Look, the Lion from the tribe of Judah, the Root of David, has conquered so that he is able to open the scroll and its seven seals" (Revelation 5:1-5, CSB).

We may have battles to fight, but God has already won the war. When Jesus died on the cross, He fulfilled that very first prophecy given back in Genesis 3. Satan struck His heel, but Jesus crushed the head of the serpent when He took back the keys to humanity and presented Himself before the Father as the perfect and ultimate sacrifice for mankind. Jesus died, but He overcame death to secure for us the victory in the war.

We see Jesus riding to battle in victory later in Revelation:

Then I saw heaven opened, and there was a white horse. Its rider is called Faithful and True, and with justice he judges and makes war. His eyes were like a fiery flame, and many crowns were on his head. He had a name written that no one knows except himself. He wore a robe dipped in blood, and his name is called the Word of God. The armies that were in heaven followed him on white horses, wearing pure white linen. A sharp sword came from his mouth, so that he might strike the nations with it. He will rule them with an iron rod. He will also trample the winepress of the fierce anger of God, the Almighty. And he has a name written on his robe and on his thigh: King of Kings and Lord of Lords" (Revelation 19:11-16, CSB).

He will come to judge, but those who are covered by His blood will not see Him as vengeful or scary. We will fall to our knees and worship the One who has always been there for us. We will shout praises to the One who humbled Himself to show us a tangible version of God. We will honor the One who saved us from destruction and gave us peace that was beyond any understanding we had. He is our promise for all eternity. Jesus, the One who is both LORD and friend, has won the war for us.

The warrior inside each of us is merely a reflection of Him. The call on our lives is to honor Him. The battles we wage aren't done by our power, but by His. And the victory we get to experience is by His blood and in His name.

Stand confidently in the woman of God you are called to be. Take up your arms to wage battle against the enemy who seeks to kill and destroy. No longer will we be content to sit back and let others fight, but we will stand side by side and back-to-back, defending our brothers and sisters in Christ, crushing the skull of the enemy one victory at a time.

REFERENCES

n.d. Puredesireministries.org.

n.d. Dohnavur Fellowship – Changing lives since 1901. Accessed December 2, 2021. https://dohnavurfellowship.org/.

"About Us." n.d. Loveworks Leadership. Accessed December 22, 2021. https://www.loveworksleadership.org/about/.

Agonito, Rosemary. n.d. "Buffalo Calf Road, Heroic Cheyenne Warrior Woman." Amazing Women In History. Accessed August 21, 2020. https://amazingwomeninhistory.com/buffalo-calf-road-cheyenne-warrior-woman/.

Brenner, M.D., Abigail. 2015. "5 Benefits of Stepping Outside Your Comfort Zone   ." Psychology Today. Psychologytoday.com/us/blog/in-flux/20512/5-benefits-stepping-outside-your-comfort-zone   .

Bristow, John T. 1988. *What Paul Really Said About Women*. New York, NY: Harper & Row.

Brown, Driver, Briggs, and Gesenius. n.d. "`ezer Meaning in Bible - Old Testament Hebrew Lexicon - King James Version." Bible Study Tools. Accessed January 20, 2022. https://www.biblestudytools.com/lexicons/hebrew/kjv/ezer-2.html.

Carswell, Roger. n.d. "The life and legacy of Amy Carmichael." Evangelical Times. Accessed December 2, 2021. https://www.evangelical-times.org/articles/historical/the-life-and-legacy-of-amy-carmichael/.

CBD News Online. 2006. "Women in the Military--International." http://web.archive.org/web/20110817105207/http://cbc.ca/news/background/military-international/.

Chrystal, Paul. 2017. *Women at War in the Classical World*. N.p.: Pen & Sword Military.

Epic Warrior Women. n.d. Episode 1, "Epic Warrior Women: Amazons Episode 1." Smithsonian Channel. Accessed May 27, 2020. https://www.smithsonianchannel.com/shows/epic-warrior-women/amazons/1004515/3437447.

"Fu Hao (fl. 1040 BCE)." 2020. Encyclopedia.com. https://www.encyclopedia.com/women/encyclopedias-almanacs-transcripts-and-maps/fu-hao-fl-1040-bce.

Gallup Inc. 2020. "Strategic Summary." Gallup. http://my.gallup.com.

Groeneveld, Emma, and Bernard Walsh. 2018. "Lagertha." World History Encyclopedia. https://www.worldhistory.org/Lagertha/.

Holland, Brynn. 2017. "Meet the Night Witches, the Daring Female Pilots Who Bombed Nazis By Night." History.com. https://www.history.com/news/meet-the-night-witches-the-daring-female-pilots-who-bombed-nazis-by-night.

James, Carolyn C. 2010. *Half the Church*. Grand Rapids: Zondervan.

"Joan of Arc - Death, Facts & Accomplishments." 2018. Biography. https://www.biography.com/military-figure/joan-of-arc.

Mark, Joshua J. 2018. "Female Gladiators in Ancient Rome." Ancient History Encyclopedias. https://www.ancient.eu/article/35.

Mark, Joshua J. 2019. "Ten Legendary Female Viking Warriors." World History Encyclopedia. https://www.worldhistory.org/article/1300/ten-legendary-female-viking-warriors/.

Mark, Joshua J. 2019. "Women in the Middle Ages." World History Encyclopedia. https://www.worldhistory.org/article/1345/women-in-the-middle-ages/.

McLelland, Kristi. 2019. *Jesus and Women in the First Century*, Session Two. Nashville: Lifeway.

Merriam-Webster.com Dictionary, s.v. "tribute," accessed May 21, 2022, https://www.merriam-webster.com/dictionary/tribute.

Mindel, Nissan. n.d. "Hagar - Jewish History." Chabad.org. Accessed August 17, 2020. http://chabad.org/library/article_cdo/aid/112053/jewish/Hagar.htm.

Morgan, Thad. 2019. "DNA Suggests Viking Women Were Powerful Warriors." History.com. http://www.history.com/news/dna-proves-viking-women-were-powerful-warriors.

Morris, Robert. 2019. *Why Am I Here? Study Guide*. N.p.: Gateway Publishing.

"Queen Amina." n.d. Encyclopedia.com. Accessed August 21, 2020. https://www.encyclopedia.com/history/news-wires-white-papers-and-books/queen-amina.

"Queen Amina: Nigerian warrior queen." n.d. BBC. Accessed August 21, 2020. https://www.bbc.com/news/av/world-africa-44888718.

Roberts, Sarah J. n.d. *Bruised Heel Society*.

"Shang Dynasty - HISTORY." 2017. History.com. https://www.history.com/topics/ancient-china/shang-dynasty.

Works, Carla. n.d. "Commentary on Matthew 15:[10-20] 21-28." Working Preacher. Accessed October 21, 2020. https://www.workingpreacher.org/preaching.aspx?commentary_id=2145.

ABOUT THE AUTHOR

Becca Ramirez is a writer and speaker called to encourage women in their identity as daughters of God and empower them to live a life that reflects that truth to the world. As a lover of learning, she immerses herself in each topic she writes and teaches. Her heart is to connect spiritual truths to our everyday lives.

When she's not at one of her kid's activities or working in the adult ministries department at her church, you'll find Becca relaxing with a giant cup of coffee and a novel. Becca, along with her husband and three kids are proud to call Fort Worth, Texas home.

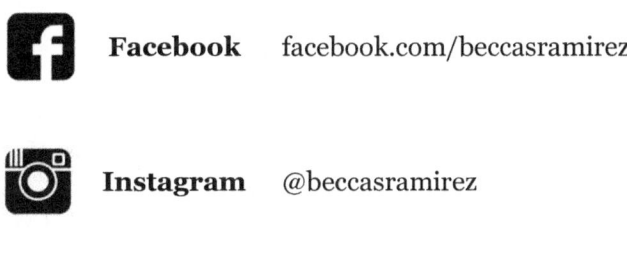

Facebook   facebook.com/beccasramirez

Instagram   @beccasramirez

TikTok   @beccasramirez